*On* WHITE FEMALE PRIVILEGE

*Catholic Reflections on Contemporary Sex*

Maximilian Hanlon

ISBN: 978-0-578-28904-5

*To all the women who have encouraged me to write this book,
and to their male allies:*

*Strive for the truth unto death, and the Lord shall fight for thee.*
(Ecclesiasticus 4:28)

# TABLE OF CONTENTS

# Chapter 1

*On Female Rapists, Feminist Hate Speech, and Fathers' Day*

When I was growing up, rape wasn't discussed as often as it is now. When the reality of rape was acknowledged, it was merely one way among many whereby men oppressed women. Although the fact that gay men sometimes rape each other was acknowledged, albeit rarely, such male-on-male rape could not be discussed without acknowledging the reality of male homosexuality, which naturally was verboten. Given how rape was conceived of and defined at that time, female-on-male and female-on-female rape was almost unintelligible, because rape required penetration of some kind, which the female body is incapable of initiating without the use of an extra-bodily implement. Consequently, for a woman to rape someone else, she would have to forcibly insert a material object into the other person's body, while the other screamed, "No, no, no!" Because no woman would ever do that, no woman could ever be a rapist.[1]

As an adult, I myself have made the acquaintance of at least a dozen rape-survivors and have listened to them with compassion as they shared with me their experiences of rape. Most of these survivors are close personal friends. Three of them were raped by women; two of the women who raped them have never been brought to justice. Every so often, one also hears of women in the news who were found guilty of the crime of rape. These cases, unfortunately, have not changed the discourse concerning rape in the requisite and desired way. For instance, when students and employees are required to watch videos that make clear what the rules regarding rape are, and what the institutional and legal consequences for rape are, we are never required to observe anyone weeping because he or she was raped by a woman and went unheard because those in power refused to acknowledge that women can be rapists. What a commitment to diversity has produced in such videos are self-narratives mostly from women and occasionally from gay men. Such rape survivors come in all shapes and sizes; they are of every possible race. One may be blind; another deaf; a third trans. But all without exception were raped by men. No one raped by a woman is given a platform from which to speak.

### The Evil of "Social Justice"

Why is this? What is the cause of the reluctance of those in power to acknowledge female-on-male and female-on-female, non-consensual sex? The answer, much to the chagrin of my opponents, is the liberal commitment to social justice. What after all is social justice? No doubt, many answers can be given to that question, but when pushed to extremes, social justice necessarily includes the privileging of the justice due to classes of oppressed persons over the justice, including punitive justice, owed to individuals. In this case, a commitment to social justice requires not punishing female rapists. The reasoning justifying such a refusal to punish might go as follows: Women collectively (i.e., every single woman without qualification) constitute a class oppressed by patriarchy. One cause of the patriarchal oppression that women are still suffering from, is the deeply ingrained belief that women cannot trust their own bodies and sexual desires. Thus, any act that reinforces the untrustworthiness of female desire, female sexuality, and the female body perpetuates patriarchy and must be opposed. But punishing female rapists publicly, as though they were no different from male predators, reinforces the historic patriarchal prejudice that female bodies (and hence, women themselves) cannot be trusted on their own to be law-compliant. Therefore, such female predators should not be punished with the same degree of punitive rigor that ought to be used to punish male rapists like Brett Cavanagh.

Perhaps a real example is required to illustrate my point. When I was in my third year of undergraduate studies, it came to my attention that a nineteen-year-old, female undergraduate raped another female student while they were both drunk. Two days or so later, the rapist admitted guilt in the dean's office and was immediately expelled from the University. If memory serves, she was also given forty-eight hours or so to move off campus completely. It should be noted that the treatment she received would have been the same if she were male. And we all knew it.

What resulted from such prompt punishment, which was blind to the gender of the miscreant? A few things are notable: (1) Even though some of my fellow students held the dean in contempt, everyone agreed that he had done the right thing. (2) None of us had any doubts that male rapists would be punished in the same way as a female offender. (3) Those who knew the victim, including me, universally responded with compassion. (4) Such public punishment fueled the religiously justified and unchecked homophobia that was institutionally taken for granted. (5) It affirmed that the female body, at its worst, is a dangerous and threatening place that must be kept in check through fear and shame. (6) It thereby affirmed that the female body is just as potentially

3

threatening as its male counterpart.

Although the response of university administration was law-compliant and transparent, liberals will no doubt dislike its effects. Because of 4, 5, and 6, such public punishment promoted both homophobia and patriarchy on campus. Consequently, such punishment also violates the canons of diversity, progress, inclusion, solidarity, and social justice. In contemporary academic discourse, however, diversity, progress, inclusion, solidarity, and social justice are sacrosanct. Therefore, all that violates them must be opposed. Plus, isn't the nineteen-year-old lesbian rapist already suffering intersectionally?

*The Good of Due Punishment*

This argument, though defective, is of interest. What would happen if all rapists were treated the same regardless of their sex or gender? And by "treated the same," I refer to both punishments at the hands of the state and institutions, and shame from the rest of us. What is the point of such punishment anyway, be it directed against male or female rapists? What good does such punishment subserve? And finally, why is the demand that male rapists be publicly punished severely an essential part of historic, feminist discourse?

In any minimally just legal system, public punishment always subserves at least two ends: (1) It seeks to cause harm of some kind to the guilty so that they at least will not commit the same crimes again. (2) It seeks to elicit fear of such punishment in the not-yet-guilty (i.e., the provisionally innocent) so that they, through fear, will abstain from crime. Notice: Punishment by definition seeks to cause harm. If the public response to misconduct does not include harming the guilty, by definition the public response does not constitute punishment, but merely correction. Now, correction is sometimes the proper way to respond to certain forms of misconduct, especially among children and young people. At other times, only punishment (i.e., intentional, retributive harm) will do. As regards rape, whether they're prepared to admit it or not, feminists have always urged that male rapists be punished and not merely corrected, so that other men, through fear of similar punishments, will resist the urge to harm women. And feminists are right to demand such punishment. If a man (i.e., a male human being who has reached the age of majority) does rape someone, he ought to be punished severely. No doubt, the fear elicited by such punishments has reduced the frequency of rape in the US.

*Too Much of a Good Thing*

What feminists perhaps do not realize is the full effects of their justified demands for punishment. It is not merely men, both guilty and innocent, who must endure the emotional burden of the fear necessary to deter crime; boys do as well. And prepubescent boys who do not yet even know what sex is, are surely innocent of rape. What happens when the anti-rape rhetoric of feminism adversely affects a boy's psychological wellbeing and understanding of his own sexuality?

I can only speak for myself. In my case, feminist rhetoric made me believe that my own body was irredeemably evil. Even before adolescence and its attendant physical changes, I was made to believe that adult responsibility for men required that all men believe that any physical attraction we might have for women merely predisposes us to harm women. This ability to cause harm was an essential part of being male that I could never change. Consequently, any male attraction to women I might

5

experience was unsalvageably threatening in a raw and irredeemable way. If I could not change the fact that I represented a threat to non-males, I could at least display guilt for the sin of merely being male.

*Feminist Man-Hating*

Feminist rhetoric clearly had a negative effect upon my upbringing. In my own case, it predisposed me to become mostly gay (which I am) and to maintain my virginity until the time of writing. If male sexuality really is as threatening and irredeemably evil as feminist rhetoric makes it seem, then the only responsible choice that a man can make is to refrain from sex with women altogether. Whether they want to admit it or not, the rhetoric of some feminists clearly does admit of this interpretation. Here, for instance, are a few cases of feminist rhetoric which clearly imply that male sexuality is irredeemably evil:

(1) The *New York Times* editorial entitled, "Men, who needs them?"[2]
(2) The book, *How to Date Men, When You Hate Men.*[3]
(3) Feminist Twitterdom claiming that Fathers' Day ought to be abolished as a legal holiday.[4]

I will now address each of these three instances of public misandry in due order:

(1) "Who needs men?" is an interesting question. First and foremost, given the important role that fathers play in the lives of their children, children need men. Second, given how men must develop friendships with other men in order to thrive as human beings, men need men. Finally, women need men. Although it is not the case that all women are heterosexual, most women are. And although it is not the case

that all heterosexual women desire sexual intimacy in their private lives and/or at least one biological child, most women do. But simple biological realities dictate that if a woman is to have heterosexual intimacy in her private life, at least one biological child, or both, a man must cooperate so that she can enjoy such good things. In short, no man, no straight sex; no man, no babies. Heterosexual women can deny that they want those things, but in fact most of them do. And yet, what have feminists instructed women to proclaim about themselves to the world? "I'm a strong woman so I don't need a man!"

As noted, not all women are heterosexual, for some women are lesbians. And presumably, being a lesbian includes preferring sexual intimacy with another woman and not with a man. I grant that. Lesbians, however, who are not batshitcrazy manhaters, typically admit that they too need men, for without friendships with men their lives would not be as complete or satisfying as they want them to be. In sum, contrary to the thrust of that editorial in the *New York Times,* one must respond to its title as follows: "Men, who needs them? Well, *you* do!"

*Woman, if you actually were strong, you would be in touch with what your desires truly are, and you would admit that if you're going to have the private life you cannot help but want, you do in fact need a man. No man, no straight sex; no man, no babies. It's just that simple. You can deny that you want one or both of those things, but if you're like most women, in fact you do.*

(2) How would the public react to a book entitled, *How to Date Black Women, When You Hate Black Women*? It goes without saying that such hate speech ought to result in serious consequences. Surely, such public acts would be met with verbal violence and justifiably so. And yet, when such venom is directed against men, no one in power, no one

whose opinions actually matter, bothers to respond with the slightest criticism.

> *Is it really so much to point out that if you hate*
> *men, your desire to date one makes no sense? If*
> *you really do want to date one of us, you can at*
> *least start by trying to hate us less.*

(3) What would happen if a conservative reactionary online agitated for the abolition of Mother's Day as a public holiday? Feminists themselves would react with a vengeance. And yet, almost no one objects to such bigotry against men. More importantly, healthy and serious relationships require that domestic partners honor one another. Even today, spouses at weddings typically do promise to try to honor one another for at least as long as their relationship might last. If, because of his radical politics, a man were to refuse to celebrate Mother's Day, he would thereby be refusing to give women, especially his wife, the honor he owes them; he would consequently be a bad husband and undeserving of his wife's love. Strange to say, as far as I know, no man has ever publicly asserted that he would refuse to celebrate Mother's Day for any reason. Even men who are divorced sometimes do celebrate the holiday for their ex-wives, if their ex-wives are the mothers of their children. I myself have heard Newt Gingrich, for instance, note with regret that his first marriage unfortunately failed, but that he still held his ex-wife in high regard, precisely because she was the mother of his children and had done her part to ensure that their children had grown up to be as happy and healthy as they could be. Despite the misfortune of the divorce, such successful parenting on her part deserved to be honored publicly. Now, Newt Gingrich admittedly has his problems, as we all do. We can criticize his politics all we want, but the fact is, by honoring his ex-wife as

he does, he is doing the right thing. Why won't feminist extremists do the same for men?

What is it that women actually want? We will return to this question later, but for now, let's affirm what should be obvious. Contrary to what the feminist orthodoxy instructs women to feel and say, most women do in fact need a man in their private lives to be as happy as they want to be. Only with the cooperation of a man can most women have the good things (i.e., long-term, emotionally satisfying, heterosexual intimacy and/or at least one biological child) they cannot help but want. If those good things, however, are to be enjoyed, spouses must be willing to make mutual sacrifices for the good of the other and to treat one another as they want to be treated. It goes without saying that if a man is making the sacrifices necessary for his spouse and children to flourish, according to the order of justice he is owed Father's Day. This is especially true, if his commitment to his family requires that he work a life-threatening and/or dehumanizing job. And yet even then, a critical mass of feminists still insists that Father's Day ought to be abolished as a civil holiday.

In short, if a woman propagates the current feminist orthodoxy regarding Father's Day, she is unworthy of male love in her private life. The due penalty for her misandry ought to be to die an unloved, untouched, childless old hag.

*No one's going after Mothers' Day. Perhaps if someone were, you would care.*

**CHAPTER 1 NOTES**

[1] To be more precise, between 1927 and 2012, The United States Department of Justice defined "forcible rape," as follows: "the carnal knowledge of a female, forcibly and against her will." Note that according to this definition, men could not be victims of rape. The broader context of the definition also required "forcible male penile penetration of a female vagina," and thus women could not be found guilty of rape. The new and current definition is broader, but insufficiently so: "The penetration, no matter how slight, of the vagina or anus with any body part or object, or oral penetration by a sex organ of another person, without the consent of the victim." (https://www.justice.gov/archives/opa/blog/updated-definition-rape) Unfortunately, this definition is still too narrow, for it requires penetration.

Other American jurisdictions maintain a more nuanced definition of sexual assault. The State of Michigan, for instance, recognizes four degrees of rape, which it prefers to term "criminal sexual conduct." The first and third degrees require penetration; the second and fourth do not. (http://www.legislature.mi.gov/(S(ppsm3b3xd1q4mp0ede3jukvf))/mileg.aspx?page=getObject&objectName=mcl-328-1931-LXXVI&highlight=rape)

[2] Greg Hampikian, "Men Who Needs Them?" *The New York Times* (August 24, 2012), https://www.nytimes.com/2012/08/25/opinion/men-who-needs-them.html

[3] Blythe Roberson, *How to Date Men When you Hate Men* (New York: Flatiron Books, 2019).

[4] Molly Wharton, "#EndFathersDay Tweets Seek to Stop Mysogynistic Celebration," *National Review* (June 13, 2014), https://www.nationalreview.com/2014/06/endfathersday-tweets-seek-stop-misogynistic-celebration-molly-wharton/

# Chapter 2
## *Cindy the Office Slut*

*Cindy the Office Slut, Part 1*

When female rapists go unpunished, and when feminist hate speech goes unacknowledged, we have important instances of the considerable privilege women continue to enjoy over men. What about sexual harassment? What happens when women in the workplace who are clearly guilty of sexual harassment, are punished less than they otherwise would be, if they were male and guilty of the same crime?

To illustrate the point: Say that I were a married man and approached for adultery by a coworker named Cindy. Say that I then do the right thing and respond with an emphatic, unambiguous, and polite *No*. However, because she was deeply wounded by men in past, failed relationships, Cindy is emotionally unstable and needy. Her neediness is unfortunately fueled by a deep-seated belief that she has never been able to overcome completely, namely that she is inherently unworthy of love. This neediness gets the better of her and, despite my *No*, she pressures me for adultery a second time. Again, I respond with an unambiguous *No* and report her to my supervisor at work, who (just for the sake of argument) is an unremarkable, conventional, white, affluent,

11

politically liberal, and privileged woman (i.e., a member of the White, Liberal Matriarchy; henceforth, WLM) who feels sorry for Cindy and, because the habitual revelation of my intellectual and moral virtue (i.e., *excellence*) at works makes her feel inferior, holds me in contempt. For the sake of this scenario, let's call my supervisor Charlotte.

Now, Cindy's behavior meets the legal definition of sexual harassment. I think it's safe to say that if I had done to Cindy what Cindy did to me, Charlotte would fire me immediately, and the cause of such professional dismissal would be publicly known. And Charlotte would enforce the rules publicly and without compassion even if she knew for certain that thereby my mental health would be destroyed and suicide would become a real possibility. I do not deny that such dismissal would be just.

To return to the scenario, say that Cindy pulls at Charlotte's heartstrings, and to help Cindy avoid suicide, Charlotte responds to me, as follows: "Max, I admit that Cindy has violated your rights. But I'm afraid that if I fire her, she'll kill herself. She's already unstable. So, I propose instead to transfer her to a different department so that you don't have to work with her anymore. Because she is already wounded and unstable, firing her would be *uncaring* and would violate our commitment to *equity* and *social justice*." How should I respond to such a supervisor at work? When social justice and individual justice conflict, which should win?

In these cases, one can expect the WLM not to act as though male and female miscreants deserve the same punishment. Two curiosities emerge here: (1) Charlotte's reactions presuppose tacit acceptance of the kind of gender-essentialism that most professional, fourth-wave feminists usually oppose. In this case, even though Cindy's behavior admittedly meets the legal definition of sexual harassment, Cindy cannot *really* be a sexual predator because Cindy is non-male. Her behavior may be unprofessional, but it cannot represent a threat to other people's welfare, like the male desire for sex. (2) Charlotte's commitment to social justice effectively denies me equal justice under law, for equal justice under law requires equal punitive justice under law. Feminists, however, have always used the demand for equal justice under law to fuel their activism, and since at least the 1980s, they have always demanded that men be punished severely for sexual harassment. But when equally severe punishments for female offenders will cause harm to the women they feel sorry for, feminists will not acquiesce to such punishments very easily.

What do women actually want? In these cases, do they want to be treated equally? Or do they want the compassion of patronizing, and hence unequal, treatment? When the two conflict, should those in power privilege solidarity with the oppressed or justice to individuals? If women actually want social justice, solidarity, and compassion when they are clearly guilty of grave crimes, why persist in maintaining the demand for equal justice under law? In the case of Cindy, equal punitive justice under law will, of course, result in the interior degradation that stems from publicly assigning guilt where guilt is due.

*Cindy the Office Slut, Part 2*

We continue with the pressing question of what women actually want. When having the conversations that contributed to this book, the reactions of women I am close to were curious. When asked how they would want their husbands to react to Cindy's overtures, they were usually inwardly conflicted in their response. To make the scenario a bit more interesting and pressing, let's add two details. Say that a *No* to Cindy will necessarily result in her suicide. Say also that a *Yes* to Cindy will result in a venereal disease being transmitted from Cindy to me and my spouse. And given that consent, at least for the purposes of our legal system, is a binary, say that in such circumstances I must respond to Cindy's offer of transgressive sex with either a *Yes* or a *No*.

When faced with the thought of their husbands in this scenario, most women I've talked to feel conflicted such that they cannot respond immediately. Strange to say, they honestly are not sure if they want their husbands to be faithful. What their delayed responses reveal is the chasm within themselves between the desire for monogamy (i.e., exclusive sexual love) and the desire for universal solidarity. At the heart of the interior conflict is American, Enlightenment, and Marxist error regarding equality. Incompatible with typically liberal sentiment is the simple reality that loving all people equally is impossible. Although we can have indefinite feelings misnamed "compassion" for countless, unknown multitudes suffering here and there, no one besides Christ Jesus can actually put love into action for all others. One must tend one's own garden, as Voltaire said.

Likewise, contrary to the permitted contours of liberal discourse, a fully human life requires a commitment to unequal loves. No one would want to live without friends, as Aristotle observed long ago,[1] but friends by definition are those we choose to love more than others (i.e., unequally). Marriage, too, is a special kind of relationship in which spouses pledge to love each other to the exclusion of all other potential sexual partners, and thus promise to love one person more than all the rest. Consequently, marital fidelity requires not merely a *Yes* to one's spouse, but a *No* to all others. What happens when that *No* causes someone else real and lasting harm? What do women want then?

Ah, the inner conflict I have observed while discussing the scenario of Cindy the Office Slut with certain fallen daughters of Eve! Although they will admit it only with reluctance, at one and the same time they want universal inclusion, class struggle, and solidarity with the oppressed, and fidelity from their husbands, monogamy, and freedom from disease. But they cannot have both! Nor are they sure if Cindy should be fired in this scenario. If doing so results in her suicide, they're honestly not sure if they want the interventionist compassion, patriarchy, and chivalry [2] necessary to save Cindy's life or the equal justice under the law that would vindicate my rights to a work environment free of sexual harassment. In the end, their exasperation renders them intellectually frigid and they fail at the project of discourse. When push comes to shove, so many university-educated women just do not know what they actually want. God save us all from such emotionally conflicted incoherence. I pity them not at a whit for their indecision.

*Cindy the Office Slut, Part 3*

I do know what I want, however. I would be faithful to my spouse even if doing so results in someone else's death. I also want my rights vindicated by seeing Cindy fired publicly for sexual harassment. If my supervisor acknowledges that Cindy's behavior meets the legal definition of sexual harassment and still refuses to fire her, a lawsuit is surely in order. Perhaps some airtime on Fox News too.

Doubtless, some feminists will react violently to my firm resolve to be faithful to my ethical commitments, which ought to be universal. Mutatis mutandis, I would, of course, expect my spouse to refuse to go whoring after an emotionally troubled coworker, for no marriage can function without a mutual commitment to monogamy. Here, however,

I must clarify the nature of the marriage bond. When I say that I will accept no sexual relationship in my private life other than a monogamous one, I mean this: I want my spouse to be willing to express his or her lifelong commitment to me by being willing, if called upon to do so in moments of temptation, to cause permanent psychological trauma to all other potential sexual partners who offer adulterous sex. Such willingness to cause others *harm* is what I want, and I refuse to alter my expectations for marriage in order to create emotionally safe places for the emotionally incontinent. Those who do not like my preferences, can go to hell. If Cindy really is so emotionally disturbed that only adultery will prevent her suicide, then she, the whole entity that she is, is not worth saving. Let the bitch die. Fuck social justice.

*The Politics of No*

But why exactly are feminists so threatened by my refusal to have sex with an emotionally troubled woman they feel sorry for? Strange to say, by making such ethical choices, I am merely doing what feminists do to men:

(1) By saying *No* to Cindy, I am exercising my right to say *No* to someone else's offer of sex. Such a right to say *No* is necessarily included in the right to bodily autonomy and self-determination that feminists have always demanded for themselves. If women are acting within their rights when they refuse to have sex with a man for any reason or no reason at all, then surely I am acting within my rights if I refuse to have sex with Cindy because such sex violates my values and religious convictions.

To illustrate: If Chelsea Clinton were to exercise her right to bodily autonomy by refusing to have sex with a black man for explicitly racist reasons (i.e., solely because he's black), the black man in question cannot legally object to her refusal. "When a woman says *No*, she means *No*," as I was frequently reminded while growing up. The right to bodily autonomy and self-determination, so cherished by professional feminists, necessarily requires that Chelsea is acting within her rights, and legally protected, if she manifests her racism in that way. Consequently, I am acting within my rights if I refuse to have sex with Cindy solely because Cindy is a crinkly-mouthed, chain-smoking, diseased, old hag. And yet, if I do openly exercise my right to say *No* for that admittedly offensive reason, the WLM will treat me like shit in retaliation.

(2) By saying *No* to Cindy, I am also exercising my right to bodily autonomy and self-determination in a way that results in the death of another human organism. But when women opt for an abortion, that is precisely what they're doing. If mainstream feminism does not object in principle to a woman's choice to abort, even for the most superficial of reasons, how can it object with any integrity to my choice to, in effect, abort Cindy? *Let the bitch die.*

(3) By refusing Cindy's offer of sex knowing that my refusal will result in her suicide, I am acting as though I do not care if my behavior increases the likelihood of suicide among women. The WLM and its allies, however, sometimes act as though they do not care if their public acts manifest brazen disregard for the lives of suicidal men. At present, the male suicide rate in the US and UK is at least three times higher than the female suicide rate.[3] And yet, mainstream, tenured feminism will not acknowledge that the male suicide rate is a problem that needs addressing. In 2013, for instance, men's-rights activists did the fundraising necessary to start the Centre for Men and Families in Toronto, which is dedicated in part to helping men avoid suicide. In response to the Centre's stated mission, Sarah Blackstock, "director of advocacy and communications at YWCA Toronto" and a

devout member of White, Liberal Matriarchy, had this to say: Men's-rights activists "tend to be more frustrated about women's rights being protected and women's equality being promoted, rather than men's rights being violated...If we're trying to build a society marked by compassion and equality, this centre [i.e., a centre dedicated in part to helping men avoid suicide] won't help us do that."[4] Especially when one realizes the extent of public-health resources then available for suffering women and their families, the Matriarchy's contempt for men prone to suicide is viscerally repulsive. Similarly, in 2015, in response to a public letter of protest signed by 200 professional feminists and their allies, the administration at the University of York publicly canceled the celebration of International Men's Day, an event dedicated in part to shedding light on the question of why the male suicide rate is so high.[5] Shockingly, but not surprisingly, the event was officially cancelled only a few hours after a male student on campus committed suicide.[6] A close examination of the letter's contents reveals the essentialism and dogmatism of such mainstream feminism: If anyone says that the sufferings of any man worldwide are in any way comparable to the sufferings of even one women anywhere, *anathema sit.* Contrary to such absolutist and easily falsifiable error, the sufferings of many men worldwide are in fact comparable to the sufferings of many women. The assertion, for example, that Chelsea Clinton is somehow necessarily more oppressed, solely in virtue of her gender, than a black, homeless, uninsured, HIV-positive, and suicidal gay man, is simply too frivolous and essentialist to be taken seriously. Such assertions completely ignore the privilege that women like Chelsea derive from their race and class. But to return to the matter at hand, if professional feminists at the University of York are acting within their rights by demanding that an academic conference dedicated in part to preventing suicide among men be cancelled, I do not see how they can assert that I am violating Cindy's rights by refusing her offer of adultery knowing that her suicide will follow.

(4) By refusing Cindy's offer of sex, I am also making the willful and informed choice not to live in solidarity with at least one suffering and oppressed person. But the fact of the matter is that mainstream feminists refuse to live in solidarity with their opponents all the time. To illustrate: Mainstream feminism typically does refuse to tolerate the presence of prolifers when they exercise their constitutional right to protest a woman's so-called "right to choose." As described in chapter 4 of this book, the tactics used to deny such protesters their rights are sometimes amusing, sometimes punctilious, and sometimes lead to verbal and physical violence. When such conflicts arise (and such conflicts are inevitable), solidarity with their opponents is not something feminists are interested in. But if feminists are acting within their rights when they respond with physical and/or verbal violence to the prolife movement, how am I failing to act within my rights, if I deny a woman solidarity by refusing her offer of sex?

*Bye-bye, Cindy*

What exactly are the issues in play here? I suppose it goes back to the Golden Rule, the ultimate principle in ethics. By refusing to have sex with Cindy when her psychological wellbeing requires a *Yes* and not a *No*, I am causing her harm, and thus doing something wrong in the eyes of my opponents. I am also offending against the imperative to create emotionally safe places *semper et ubique* for women who are suffering. Although they will not admit it openly, viscerally my opponents also believe that by refusing her offer, I am doing something that ideally I should be criticized for. And if it were politically expedient to do so, they would put limits on my right to say *No* in such circumstances.

Such a response necessarily follows from the errors of moral relativism and consequentialism. On the one hand, we have an emotionally unstable woman who needs help to avoid suicide; on the other, we have my desire not to commit adultery and not to spread her disease to my spouse and myself. Because a woman's suicide is arguably worse than the spread of venereal disease via adultery, the consequentialist must urge me to commit adultery to help Cindy avoid suicide. Nevertheless, by refusing to accept my choice that will bring about Cindy's death, my critics are seeking to impose limitations on at least one person's right to bodily autonomy. Such criticisms are unacceptable and ought to be met with caustic retaliation. In this case, if my behavior does result in Cindy's suicide, not only am I acting within my rights by refusing to have sex with her; others are violating my rights if they come to Cindy's defense.

*If you are so psychologically fucked up that only adultery will prevent your suicide, you, the whole entity that you are,*
*are not worth saving. God thinks so too.*

**CHAPTER 2 NOTES**

[1] Aristotle, *Nicomachean Ethics* 8.1, 1155a5.

[2] Yes, chivalry is a form of patriarchy, which, contrary to what they *say*, women both do and do not want.

[3] https://webappa.cdc.gov/sasweb/ncipc/mortrate.html;https://www.ons.gov.uk/peoplepopulationandcommunity/birthsdeathsandmarriages/deaths/bulletins/suicidesintheunitedkingdom/2017registrations.

[4] Alex Nino Gheciu, "Controversial Men's Rights Group Fundraising for a Centre for Men and Families," *The Star* (August 15, 2013), https://www.thestar.com/news/gta/2013/08/15/controversial_mens_rights_group_fundraising_for_a_centre_for_men_and_families.html.

[5] For the letter, see https://nouse.co.uk/2015/11/16/open-letter-blasts-universitys-decision-to-mark-international-mens-day-read-it-here/. For the administration's response, see https://www.york.ac.uk/news-and-events/news/2015/events/mensday-gender-equality/.

[6] Milo Yiannopoulos, "Male University of York Student Commits Suicide on Day his University Ditches International Men's Day after Pressure from Feminists," *Breitbart* (November 18, 2015), https://www.breitbart.com/the-media/2015/11/18/male-university-of-york-student-commits-suicide-on-day-his-university-ditches-international-mens-day-after-pressure-from-feminists/

# Chapter 3
## Feminist Promotion of the Rape Culture

*Feminist Deformation and Rape Porn*

If we take a step back from the scenario and consider the implications of such subliminal rhetoric, however, it is almost amusing to note that my liberal critics' inward criticism of my chastity reveals their urge to perpetuate the rape culture. Unlike some conservatives, I do acknowledge that the rape culture actually exists and that we must talk about it to reduce its dehumanizing effects upon actual and potential victims. Contrariwise, with certain radical forms of feminism, I assert that mainstream feminism has also done its part to promote the rape culture. [1] Such feminist rape promotion requires deeper analysis.

When the informed observer surveys the development of feminism's four waves, its historical trajectory is initially almost unthinkable. The transmogrification of second-wave, sex-negative, snooty-nosed, venomous, aggressive librarian ladies with horn-rimmed eyewear held on their heads by slender chains, who condemned pornography and prostitution as intolerable means of perpetuating patriarchy, into gender-queer, sexually liberated, activist types bringing children to drag-queen story hour at the local library is both unexpected and disturbing. What is also disturbing is the cultural and financial privilege of third- and fourth-wave feminists who insist that pornography and prostitution can actually be a form of liberation for women. Perhaps that's the subjective experience of a tiny number of women of their own class, but for the vast majority of women worldwide pornography is clearly bad. Only when one realizes that by 2007 at least 40% of young men aged 18–25 had seen pornographic images online of women being raped, tortured, and/or murdered does one catch a whiff of the full extent of the contemporary depravity and perversion that mainstream feminism actively promotes.[2] No doubt, fifteen years later that number must be higher. Surely, we can all see that rape porn is bad for women; it is also bad for men. And it surely feeds the rape culture.

More important than rape porn, however, is the feminist response to outspoken feminists who are guilty of rape. Arguably, the most famous case of female-on-male rape in our own time is that of Anna Stubblefield, professional feminist and academic fraud. Her case was widely reported in the mainstream media and has been conveniently summarized, as follows:[3]

> *Newark*—Acting Essex County Prosecutor Carolyn A. Murray announced today that the Honorable Siobhan Teare, Judge of the Superior Court, has sentenced the former Chairwoman of the Rutgers University Philosophy Department to 12 years in New Jersey State Prison for repeatedly sexually assaulting a disabled man in her school office.

> Authorities said on Oct. 2, 2015 an Essex County jury convicted Marjorie Anna Stubblefield, 46, of West Orange of two counts of first degree aggravated sexual assault for repeatedly engaging in sexual acts with a man

suffering from cerebral palsy who was unable to speak or communicate.

The victim wears a diaper and requires assistance with basic needs such as eating, walking, and bathing, and has the mental capacity of a toddler.

Today, Stubblefield was sentenced to 12 years in New Jersey State Prison. Under the No Early Release Act, she must serve 85 percent of her sentence before she is eligible for parole. In addition, she will have to register under Megan's Law when she is released from prison and she has been disqualified from public employment.

Assistant Prosecutor Eric Plant, who tried the case, said, "Professor Stubblefield was a trusted and respected member of the university community who used her position to prey on the victim. What she did was not only criminal, it was cruel. Knowing how desperately families of disabled individuals are for some hope, she mislead the victim's family into believing that she was making progress in helping their son to communicate while all the while she was simply satisfying her own tawdry desires. In the process, she did great damage to this young man, his family, and even her own family."

Stubblefield admitted taking him out of the wheel chair, putting him on the floor in her office, removing his diaper, and performing oral sex on the victim on one occasion. She admitted engaging in vaginal intercourse at her Rutgers University office, where she was allegedly teaching him to communicate through something known as facilitated communication, a controversial and discredited method of communicating.

Stubblefield met the victim in 2009 when his brother took her class. During the class she showed a video on facilitated communication. After viewing the video, the victim's brother asked if she thought his brother could be taught this method of communications.

From 2009 to 2011, Stubblefield worked with the victim. She took him from his home to her office. She also met him at a day program. Eventually she started taking him to conferences where she presented him as evidence of the effectiveness of facilitated communications. She claimed he wrote complicated term papers and essays and expressed high level thinking.

She even took him on a date in New York City where she claimed he told her she should not drink wine because she was the designated driver. After awhile the victim's family members became concerned because they were unable to communicate with him despite her claims that he was typing and communicating.

Eventually, she confessed to the family that she

was in love with the victim and planning to leave her husband and children to live in an apartment with the victim.

At that point, the victim's mother and brother, who had been appointed by the court to serve as legal guardians, asked her to stay away from the victim.

Despite their request, she continued to try to make contact with the victim, causing the family to contact the University. Given the nature of the allegations, the University contacted authorities and Stubblefield was arrested and charged following a lengthy investigation.

During the trial, experts testified that the victim was legally incompetent, unable to communicate and thus unable to consent to sex. In addition, the evidence showed that facilitated communication has been discredited as a valid method of communications.

At trial, Professor James Todd, a psychology professor at Eastern Michigan University, said facilitated communication had become "the single most scientifically discredited intervention in the entire discipline of developmental disabilities."[4]

A few additional details are pertinent to us here: (1) Despite her self-serving convictions to the contrary, Stubblefield knew that facilitated communication (henceforth,

FC) was regarded as pseudoscience by most of the academic community. Although her supposed academic background is in philosophy, not in one of the hard sciences, she persisted in the error that the scientific consensus regarding FC is not to be trusted. Indicative of the liberal commitment to censorship, in 2011 she labeled the legitimate science demonstrating the unreliability of FC *hate speech*:

> Anti-FC rhetoric functions not as principled scientific debate intended to help humanity in its quest for truth but rather as hate speech intended to silence dissenters, with the result (whether intended or not) of contributing to the ongoing marginalization and oppression within our society of people labeled as intellectually impaired.[5]

Unfortunately, *hate speech* does exist and it often deserves explicit censorship, but liberal misuse of the term now serves more often than not to censor the very discourses that institutions, universities, and governments are obligated to have. Naturally, there is at present no universally agreed upon definition of the term.

(2) There can be no doubt that Stubblefield did not merely rape her victim; she first turned him into a puppet and made him play the role of her ideal lover:

> Other things raised Wesley's [the victim's brother and legal guardian] suspicions, too. Some of D.J.'s [i.e., the victim] messages didn't seem as if they came from him. D.J. typed with Anna that he didn't like gospel music, but Wesley knew his brother loved to sway in church, doing what Wesley called the "Stevie

Wonder dance." D.J. also typed, through Anna, that he enjoyed red wine—especially from a label called Fat Bastard. But Wesley spent Communion Sundays with D.J. and said he never showed much interest in drinking wine. "It seemed very class-based," Wesley said. "It seemed very much of what she liked but not what [D.J.] liked."

...Anna asked him [D.J.] if he might want to see some pornography, "to see what things looked like and different positions people used and that sort of thing." She said she wouldn't want to pay for porn or watch anything offensive, but that she would be O.K. with finding free clips on the Internet that depicted couples engaging in mutually pleasurable intercourse. He demurred, typing out that in his view the women in porn are being exploited, and that, besides, Anna was more beautiful than any porn star, and he really wanted to be thinking only about her when they finally made love.[6]

(3) Despite being a professional social justice warrior and anti-racist, Stubblefield revealed a deep-seated racism towards D.J.'s family:

[Wesley] cast his complaint in terms that harked to Anna's scholarship in racial justice: "Her continued attempts to see [D.J.] and her insinuation that my mother and I do not know what is in [D.J.'s] best interest is insulting and straddles the racial assumptions about the capacity of black parents to properly raise their children." He had accused Anna of turning into her own worst nightmare. "White people uphold white privilege in ways that they repress," she once wrote. [7] Even when they mean to help, they behave "in ways that are disrespectful and that undermine the self-empowerment of the people whose space they invade." Had Anna done the same to D.J. and his family? A professor of ethics who wrote passionately about the rights of the disabled was accused of sexually assaulting the person she was most determined to protect—a black, disabled man; a child of a single mother; a member of the most vulnerable among the vulnerable. [8]

Race naturally plays a crucial role in the case. The judge, Siobhan Teare, is a black woman and was thus in a position to do justice for the black victim. [9] She did her duty by imposing the penalty for rape required by law without regard for the mental health of the white, privileged, sexually violent, and feminist miscreant. The charge was "for two counts of first-degree aggravated sexual assault, the same charge that would apply to someone who had inflicted severe injury during a rape or participated in a violent gang rape." [10] When the jury delivered its guilty verdict, Judge Teare called Stubblefield "'the perfect example of a predator preying on her prey.' Now [the Judge] gave the sentence: Anna would get 12 years in prison. The first 10 years, 2 months and 13 days would be served with no possibility of parole." "Anna sat in silence as her lawyers argued for continuation of her $100,000 bail. When the judge explained that Anna had been convicted of two counts of a first-degree felony and that further bail would be impossible, she collapsed onto the defense table in loud, convulsive sobs. 'Please,' she begged, 'what about my daughter?'[11] Judge Teare persisted and justice was served when Stubblefield was taken out of the courtroom in handcuffs and shame without the possibility of parole.[12]

*Liberal Responses to Feminist-Endorsed Rape*

Curiously, a critical mass of supporters came to Stubblefield's defense. Their arguments reveal their belief that Stubblefield was somehow not really guilty, or the sentence was too harsh, or both, or some other form of incoherent dribble. Here, for instance, is the essential part of Peter Singer's and Jeff McMahan's objections to Judge Teare's ruling that appeared in *The New York Times*:

> A central issue in the trial was whether D.J. is profoundly cognitively impaired, as the prosecution contended and the court seemed to accept, or is competent cognitively but unable to communicate his thoughts without highly skilled assistance, as the defense contended. If we assume that he is profoundly cognitively impaired, we should concede that he cannot understand the normal significance of sexual relations between persons or the meaning and significance of sexual violation. These are, after all, difficult to articulate even for persons of normal cognitive capacity. In that case, he is incapable of giving or withholding informed consent to sexual relations; indeed, he may lack the concept of consent altogether.
>
> This does not exclude the possibility that he was wronged by Stubblefield, but it makes it

less clear what the nature of the wrong might be. It seems reasonable to assume that the experience was pleasurable to him; for even if he is cognitively impaired, he was capable of struggling to resist, and, for reasons we will note shortly, it is implausible to suppose that Stubblefield forcibly subdued him. On the assumption that he is profoundly cognitively impaired, therefore, it seems that if Stubblefield wronged or harmed him, it must have been in a way that he is incapable of understanding and that affected his experience only pleasurably.

If, by contrast, we assume that he has normal cognitive capacities, certain uncontested facts make it difficult to believe that he was forced to have sex against his will—for example, that he cooperated in the process of revealing to his family that he and Stubblefield had had sexual relations. On the assumption that he has normal cognitive abilities, he would surely have found a way to express his hostility to Stubblefield on        that       occasion    or subsequently. Evidence of such hostility would have strengthened the prosecution's case. The prosecution, however, offered no evidence that D.J. had ever shown hostility to Stubblefield.[13]

Naturally, the authors of such sex-positive bullshit are "professional ethicists" and tenured faculty at Princeton and Oxford. Their "arguments" boil down to the following: If D.J. is severely impaired, it is at least probable that he was not aware of being harmed by Stubblefield. Because there is no indication that he objected to the sex, because he was not aware of being harmed, and because he probably found the sex pleasurable, if he was "raped," the "rape" wasn't all that bad. By extension, so long as children, the disabled, and those asleep do not object to sex, (non-consensual) sex with them may not be objectionable if such sex maximizes their pleasure.

Of course, the responses to Singer's and McMahan's editorial and to Stubblefield's conduct in general were mixed. Some took the cowardly approach and responded with a cool and distant "objectivity."[14] Many responded in ways that were intended to be openly divisive, and thereby did their duty to shame their opponents.[15] But what really is going on here? Why the reluctance to condemn Stubblefield in accordance with her demerits? Here, I will review a few reasons that are indicative of radical defects in the liberal intellect.

*Liberal Preference for Pseudoscience*

(1) The Left rejects science when the results of legitimate science conflict with their emotional reactions to things. When I was growing up, it was the Right that was usually characterized as anti-intellectual and anti-science because of the Right's association with biblical fundamentalists' rejection of modern evolutionary theory. More recently, the Right is notorious for its opposition to the legitimate science proving that climate change is the result of human activity. Surprisingly, however, the Left rejects the legitimate results of science just as often, but typically goes uncriticized for it in the mainstream media. The conflict between Leftists in the humanities and politically neutral scientists has been documented at some length elsewhere.[16]

Here, I shed light on similar liberal proclivities that reveal a deep-seated aversion to science. A critical mass of liberal hippy-types, for instance, persist in believing in homeopathy despite the fact that homeopathy has been proven to be pseudoscience many times over. Those who believe that crystals have magic powers are equally contemptible. As I'm fond of pointing out, belief in crystals and homeopathy (i.e., magic potions) amounts to witchcraft. And despite the scientific consensus regarding both errors, those who believe in them often display fundamentalist fervor to their favorite kinds of superstition.

> *Hate it or love: If all hippies are liberal, some liberals are hippies. And yes, traditional modes of logic are universally binding, even if the mandatory nature of traditional logic constitutes a form of patriarchal and Eurocentric oppression.*

More importantly, the liberal itch for postmodernism in history and literature ultimately contradicts the presuppositions not only of modern natural science, but also of mathematics. The latter two disciplines presuppose that certain kinds of human thinking are universally valid regardless of the race, class, gender, or identity of the thinker. The presupposition, however, that some arguments are valid independently of anyone's identity, such that consideration of the thinker's identity is ultimately a distraction from the argument itself, is precisely what postmodernism rejects. Thus, the recent scourge of liberal academics, like Laurie Rubel of Brooklyn College, claiming that 2+2=4 "reeks of White supremacist patriarchy" and their falsifiable and factually inaccurate bullshit.[17] A similar case would be liberal opposition to the spread of Western medicine in non-Western cultural contexts, despite the fact that Western medicine routinely prevents deaths that would otherwise be common.[18] Indeed, as any Western-trained physician who has worked or done volunteer service in Africa can tell you, Western medicine prevents women from dying in childbirth; the superstitions and witchcraft of African shamans and witchdoctors do not. Another example more pertinent to the contemporary US would be the fat acceptance movement, which rejects the scientific fact that obesity is always bad for one's health. I grant that obesity in some cultures is sometimes considered beautiful or might indicate high class or social status. I also grant that some people find fat people sexually attractive.[19] Neither of those facts, however, negates the simple biological reality that excessive fat is always unhealthy. If that more important fact hurts some people's feelings, they need to get the fuck over it.

*Science should trump and displace feelings.*
*Yes, even **your** feelings.*

*Making Mommy Cry*

As regards the Stubblefield case, the legitimate science against FC is rock solid. And yet her supporters dogmatically believe in it anyway. Why is this? Two explanations present themselves, one noble, the other ignoble, both emotionally disordered: (1) Some who (wrongly) believe in FC do so, because it gives them what they deeply want, viz., the ability to communicate with their disabled loved ones who are otherwise consigned to the prison of disabled speechlessness. This admittedly noble desire is understandable, but still grounded in unadulterated error. (2) Those who pigheadedly believe in FC do so, because the alternative would require that they condemn and shame a woman they like and feel sorry for. But why are they reluctant to condemn and shame Stubblefield? The reasons are both emotional, and upon reflection have grave political consequences:

(a) Initially and emotionally, punishing Stubblefield as

though she represents just as much of a threat to other people's welfare as a male predator, requires that those in power go out of their way to cause a woman real, demonstrable harm, and to take positive steps to make someone's mommy cry. It means not altering our behavior, even if we have good reason to think that such punishment will result in her suicide. Justice in these cases requires raw punishment. And by punishment, I mean the potentially permanent destruction of the female rapist's mental health *usque ad mortem.* And justice in these cases also requires systematically disregarding one's subrational emotional reactions when such emotions interfere with the imposition of a purely punitive justice. I hold as well that the death penalty is morally required in cases like hers.

*Control your cunt, bitch, or burn in hell.*

(b) Politically, Stubblefield's guilt requires punishing a well-liked and woke member of the ruling class for trusting her body and her feelings, and for pursuing the sex she had to have in order to be happy. What really has Stubblefield done? Just like Thomas Jefferson, she grasped at the forbidden fruit of prohibited sex, i) because she sincerely believed the sex was ethical; (ii) because (she at least thought) it was required for her happiness; and (iii) because she had good reason to think that no one would punish her for it. Such punishment, however, conflicts with the quintessentially American claim that the pursuit of happiness is the most basic human right there is. My rejection of such Jeffersonian and Americanist dogma requires more explanation.

\

*When Women Should not be Trusted*

The liberal position on women's rights typically goes as follows: If a woman feels that an abortion is ethical, then the rest of us are legally and ethically obligated to trust her and to provide her with access to an abortion. If a woman feels that she's a man, then the rest of us are legally and ethically obligated to trust her and to act as though she were a man. If a woman feels that a given act of sex is rape, then the rest of us are legally and ethically obligated to trust her, and to punish the accused (and presumably male) rapist, solely because she says he's guilty. Likewise, if a woman feels that a given instance of sex is *not* rape, presumably the rest of us are obligated not to object to her lusts and violent perversion. The only thing that matters is how the woman in question *feels*; such *feelings* are simply per se infallible and cannot be wrong.

*Fuck your feelings, bitch; they're not real.*

But if Stubblefield is guilty, then we have an important exception to that general rule. For here we are justified in punishing a woman severely solely because of the way she *feels* and her poor choice to act in light of her feelings. With such a legal precedent, the door naturally opens to disregarding the (similarly disordered and irrational) feelings of some other women (and of some men too) by punishing them severely for trusting themselves and pursuing happiness, as they see fit. "Equal rights" for trans people are naturally at stake here. So is "a woman's right to choose" and the proper way to respond to an accusation of rape.

The potential political ramifications of the case go deeper (pun intended). For when Stubblefield raped D.J., she was merely pursuing her happiness. And her happiness supposedly requires a certain kind of sex. Therefore, denying her her preferred mode of sex is to deny her the most basic of all rights claimed by Americans, viz., the right to pursue happiness. Such reasoning has been at the heart of the Left's support of the sexual revolution since the push for birth control in the 1950s. In sum:

> *Every single human being has the right to pursue happiness.*
> *Pursuing happiness requires the freedom to pursue one's preferred mode of sex.*
> **Ergo,** *every single human being has the right to pursue his/her preferred mode of sex.*

If we apply this general principle to the case at hand, we have:

> (1) *Anna Stubblefield is a human being.*
> **Ergo,** *Anna Stubblefield has the right to pursue her preferred mode of sex.*

> (2) *Anna Stubblefield's preferred mode of sex is with black, mute quadriplegics.*
> **Ergo,** *Anna Stubblefield has the right to pursue sex with black, mute quadriplegics.*

What changes, however, in this quintessentially American paradigm if we are justified in punishing at least one American with the death penalty precisely because she grasped at the sex she had to have in order to be happy? And notice: There is at least one such American who deserves that punishment. And that American is a woman.

*Thomas Jefferson: Father of the American Rape Culture*

Notice also that I have identified the right to pursue

happiness by pursuing one's preferred mode of sex *Jeffersonian*. I have done so quite intentionally, not merely because the claim that there is a right to the pursuit of happiness derives from The Declaration of Independence, but also because Jefferson himself embodied that right through adulterous rape in his private life. Although Anna Stubblefield's class denied it for decades, modern scholarship has brought to light the fact that Jefferson did father the children of Sally Hemings, his slave. Notice: Regardless of the ethical standards we use to judge him, Jefferson is guilty of grave misconduct. If we judge him according to the standards of his time, he is guilty of habitual fornication (i.e., of habitually having sex with a woman who was not his wife). If we judge him according to the standards of our time, he is guilty of multiple rapes, for slaves by definition do not have the right to refuse to have sex with their owners. But if they do not have the right to refuse, they cannot consent either. Jefferson's perversion and the perversion of other white, Southern slave owners is particularly revolting, because their refusal to give up the rape they had to have in order to be happy, caused their refusal to let their slaves go free; their refusal to let the slaves go free, caused the Civil War. And all because they refused to control their dicks.

In sum, Stubblefield plus Jefferson gives us proof that when left to their own devices, certain Americans, both in our own time and in times past, will naturally pursue their happiness by (at least attempting to) rape. Some such Americans are men; others are women; all are equally guilty not merely for *doing* something wrong, but more importantly, for merely *being* the worthless pieces of shit they are. Because they cannot be trusted not to rape, at the core of their being they are not equal to the rest of us who can be trusted not to pursue our happiness in that way. Because they are not equal, they do not deserve equal rights. And when they are caught red-handed pursuing their happiness through rape, they ought to be executed by the State for their perversion. Hence, because the American Civil War was merely the punishment due to the crime and sin of rape that Jefferson and his spiritual descendants enjoyed and defended, the bloody violence of the Civil War and its outcome were both legitimate and just.

We are not all equal. And some of us (including me) at least some of the time are qualified to make the judgment as to who is not equal. Of course, those of Jefferson's and Stubblefield's class do not want to hear the simple fact that because of their moral degeneracy, they deserve neither equal rights nor power. But that's just a function of their own perversion and refusal to take responsibility for their own foul moral character.

*Control your dick, asshole;*
*control your cunt, bitch, or burn in hell.*

*Getting Racist Mommy Off the Hook*

Unfortunately, in 2017 Stubblefield's sentence was reversed on appeal.[20] The appellate court ruled that because Stubblefield was not allowed to present evidence in her defense that lent credence to FC, she deserved a new trial. The appellate court also insisted that the case be assigned to a different judge. As described in *The New York Times:*

> Anna's original conviction has been erased; the judge who sentenced her to serve a dozen years in prison, and denounced her as "the perfect example of a predator preying on their prey," was reassigned from the case; and the prosecutor's office agreed to let her go with

time served. (D.J.'s family was awarded a $4 million judgment in a civil suit, but Anna does not appear to have the means to pay it.)[21]

A few things must be noted about such an unfortunate turn of events: (1) The appellate court's decision rejects Judge Teare's judgment that testimony in support of FC is not permissible evidence, because the scientific consensus against FC is rock solid. Consequently, the door opens for other forms of pseudoscience to be permitted as evidence in courts of law. (2) Of the three judges who served on the court of appeals, two (Susan L. Reisner and Ellen Koblitz) are devout members of the WLM. Of course, because they are members of the WLM, they cannot be trusted to punish another White Liberal Matriarch for pursuing the kind of sex she has to have in order to be happy. (3) By showing mercy to the white rapist, the WLM manifested its racism by openly disregarding the testimony of most of the blacks involved in the case. In his official correspondence with the court, Roger Stubblefied, Anna's black ex-husband, described her, as follows:

> I do believe that Anna is a pathological liar and narcissistic...I believe it possible that given any opportunity she would definitely repeat the effort to pose herself as Anne Sullivan to Helen Keller, or perhaps a martyr like Anne Frank. She will stop at nothing to fool the court and seek vindication, regardless of the emotional and financial expense to her family or the primary victim's family.[22]

Likewise, D.J.'s mother openly accused the court of racism in the press:

"Look at him, he can't consent," D.J.'s mother told me when last week's hearing ended. D.J., who was present with his brother and his brother's pregnant wife, is roughly five feet tall, and he is mostly quiet but for grunts and chirps. "You call that justice?" she continued. "Print this in *The New York Times.* Tell them what the mother said: A white woman did this to my son."

She didn't have to spell it out; the racial context for the plea was clear enough. If the roles had been reversed—if the victim had been a small, white woman in a diaper who could not speak or dress herself, and if the defendant had been a black man in a position of authority—would things have ended this way?[23]

## Professional Fraud

One final note on this sordid affair: Earlier in this chapter, I called Stubblefield an *academic fraud.* Here, I justify that assertion. Happily, because of the constraints of modern university life, Stubblefield's doctoral dissertation is available through the Dissertation Abstracts (also called ProQuest Dissertations and Theses) database to anyone who can access it. [24] A few embarrassing details immediately reveal themselves to the inquirer. Her dissertation is only 124 pages long and contains an improperly formatted bibliography of only three pages. For those of us who have completed doctoral dissertations in the humanities that are authentic, precisely because they do not merely regurgitate passed scholarship in light of one's own feelings, 124 pages is merely three term papers copied and pasted together. A bibliography of only three pages is likewise laughably inadequate.

Curiously, one factor that all her sources have in common is pertinent to us here: All are written in English. Stubblefield's mode of doing scholarship testifies to a peculiarly American form of colonialism that in professional social justice warriors like her almost always remains oblivious to the racist herself. Such persons believe that they are not under any obligation to even try to learn a single foreign language to an advanced level; thereby, they reveal their colonial expectations that the rest of the world learn English. This ignorance of foreign languages for which American academics are internationally notorious is particularly unacceptable in the current climate in which serious academic work must usually involve intercultural exchange. Without foreign language acquisition, intercultural exchange on equal terms with people outside the Anglosphere is impossible.

Anna Stubblefield is a professional fraud, a convicted rapist, and deeply racist. And yet she not only had tenure at Rutgers; she served as the head of the philosophy department. How can this be? Why does the American university system hire such sexually depraved and violent, grossly incompetent, unqualified, and silly bitches? WHITE, FEMALE PRIVILEGE, I suppose, has everything to do with it. Let it not be said that "no one will ever read your dissertation." If I'm out to prove you're a fraud, I will.

*Would someone please explain to me why that bitch has my job?*
*She's a fraud.*

**CHAPTER 3 NOTES**

[1] For two examples of a mainstream feminist promoting and defending rape porn, see Heather Murphy, "New Scrutiny for Men who Rape," *The New York Times* D1 (October 31, 2017), published online as "What Experts Know about Men who Rape," https://www.nytimes.com/2017/10/30/health/men-rape-sexual-assault.html; and Tracy Clark-Flory, "In Defense of 'Rape' Fantasies," November 21, 2013, https://www.salon.com/2013/11/20/in_defense_of_rape_fantasies/. For one radical feminist's perfectly reasonable and salutary condemnation of Clark-Flory's degrading perversion, see Meghan Murphy, "xHamster's Fake Ethics Won't Stop Rape or Rape Culture," *Feminist Current* (June 30, 2016), https://www.feministcurrent.com/2016/06/30/xhamster-joins-ranks-porn-companies-trying-fake-ethics/. For examples of violent crime caused in part by rape porn, see, Joan Smith, "The Truth about Men who Watch Violent Porn—And How Dangerous They Are to Women," *The Telegraph* (November 12, 2015), https://www.telegraph.co.uk/women/life/violent-porn-dangers-posed-to-women/.

[2] Patrizia Romito and Lucia Beltramini, "Watching Pornography: Gender Differences, Violence and Victimization: An Exploratory Study in Italy," *Violence Against Women* 17, issue 10 (October 2011): 1313–1326. For more of this study in context, see Miranda A. H. Horvath, Llian Alys, Kristina Massey, Afroditi Pina, Mia Scally, and Joanna R. Adler, "'Basically...Porn Is Everywhere': A Rapid Evidence Assessment on the Effects That Access and Exposure to Pornography Has on Children and Young People," Office of the Children's Commissioner, https://www.mdx.ac.uk/__data/assets/pdf_file/0026/48545/BasicallyporniseverywhereReport.pdf.

[3] For some of the coverage of the trial, see the following: Thomas Zambito, "Rutgers-Newark Philosophy Chairwoman Fights Criminal Sexual Assault Charges," April 20, 2014, https://www.nj.com/news/2014/04/chairwoman_of_rutgers-newark_philosophy_department_fighting_criminal_sexual_assault_charges_involvin.html; Bill Wichert, "Rutgers Professor Accused of Sexual Assault Fights to Bar Document from Trial," December 11, 2014, https://www.nj.com/essex/2014/12/rutgers_professor_accused_of_sexually_assaulting_mentally_disabled_man_fights_to_bar_document_from_t.html; Daniel Engber, "The Strange Case of Anna Stubblefield," *The New York Times Magazine,* October 20, 2015, https://www.nytimes.com/2015/10/25/magazine/the-strange-case-of-anna-stubblefield.html; Bill Wichert, "Judge OKs Document Detailing Rutgers Professor's Sexual Relations with Mentally Disabled Man," January 8, 2015, https://www.nj.com/essex/2015/01/judge_approves_document_use_in_trial_of_rutgers_professor_accused_of_sexually_assaulting_mentally_di.html; Bill Wichert, "Judge Sets Rules for Professor's Testimony at Sex Assault Trial," August 13, 2015, https://www.nj.com/essex/2015/08/judge_sets_rules_for_rutgers_

professors_testimony.html; Bill Wichert, "Jury Selection to Begin in Rutgers Professor's Sex Assault Trial," August 25, 2015, https://www.nj.com/essex/2015/08/jury_selection_to_begin_in_ rutgers_professors_sex.html; Bill Wichert, "Is Professor Using 'Ouiji Board' Science to Defend Herself in Sex Abuse Case?" September 9, 2015, https://www.nj.com/essex/2015/09/advocates_critics_debate_communicati on_technique_i.html#incart_river; Bill Wichert, "Professor Goes on Trial in Alleged Sexual Abuse of Disabled Man," September 10, 2015, https://www.nj.com/essex/2015/09/rape_or_love_professor_goes_on_trial_ in_alleged_ab.html; Bill Wichert, "Professor, Accused of Sex Assault, Declares Love for Disabled Man," September 11, 2015, https://www.nj.com/essex/2015/09/professor_accused_of_sex_assault_decl ares_love_for.html#incart_river; Bill Wichert, "Professor Engaged in 'Twisted Fantasy' of Sex with Disabled Man, Witness Says," September 16, 2015,https://www.nj.com/essex/2015/09/professor_engaged_in_twisted_fa ntasy_of_sex_with_d.html; Bill Wichert, "Professor Accused of Bruising Disabled Man During Sex Assault," September 17, 2015, https://www.nj.com/essex/2015/09/professor_accused_of_causing_abrasio ns_on_disabled.html; Bill Wichert, "Professor Rejects Claim she 'Raped" Disabled Man," September 25, 2015, https://www.nj.com/essex /2015/09/professor_rejects_claim_she_raped_disabled_man.html#incart_st ory_package; Bill Wichert, "Jury Begins Deliberations in Professor's Sex Assault Trial," October 1, 2015, https://www.nj.com/essex/2015/10/ jury_begins_deliberations_in_professors_sex_assaul.html; Bill Wichert, "Prosecturos Challenge Controversial Technique in Professor's Sex Assault Trial," October 1, 2015, https://www.nj.com/essex/ 2015/10/prosecutors_challenge_controversial_technique_in_p.html#incart _story_package; Bill Wichert, "Professor Found Guilty of Sexually Assaulting Disabled Man," October 2, 2015, https://www.nj.com/essex /2015/10/professor_found_guilty_of_sexually_assaulting_disa.html#incart _river_home; Bill Wichert, "Juror Explains Why Professor was Convicted of Sexually Assaulting Disabled Man," October 3, 2015, https://www.nj.com/essex/2015/10/why_was_professor_convicted_of_sex ual_assaulting_d.html; RLS Staff, "Former Chairwoman of Rutgers University Philosophy Department Sentenced to 12 Years for Raping Disabled Man," January 15, 2016, https://www.rlsmedia.com/article/ former-chairwoman-rutgers-university-philosophy-department-sentenced -12-years-raping; Bill Wichert, "Convicted Professor's Jailhouse Letter: I Loved Disabled Man," January 24, 2016, https://www.nj.com/ essex/2016/01/in_jailhouse_letter_professor_convicted_of_sex_ass.html; Thomas Moriarty, "Rutgers Prof Convicted in Sex Assault of Disabled Man Ordered to Pay $4M," October 25, 2016, https://www.nj.com/essex/2016 /10/judge_awards_4_million_to_family_of_anna_stubblefi.html; Nick Rummell, "Ex-Professor Convicted of Raping Disabled Man Gets New Trial," Courthouse News Service, June 9, 2017, https://www. courthousenews.com/ex-professor-convicted-raping-disabled-man-gets-new-trial/; Colleen Flaherty, "Second Chance for Fallen Philosopher," June 12, 2017, https://www.insidehighered.com/news/2017/06/12/professor-accused-raping-disabled-man-sees-her-convictions-overturned; Daniel Engber, "A Second Chance for Anna Stubblefield," June 14, 2017, https://slate.com/technology/2017/06/the-conviction-in-the-anna-stubblefield-facilitated-communication-case-has-been-overturned.html; Daniel Engber, "The Strange Case of Anna Stubblefield, Revisited," *The New York Times Magazine,* April 15, 2018, https://www.nytimes.com /2018/04/05/magazine/the-strange-case-of-anna-stubblefield-revisited. html; and Alex Napoliello, "No More Prison for Ex-Rutgers Professor who Sexually Assaulted Disabled Student," January 30, 2019,https:// www.nj.com/essex/2018/05/anna_stubblefield_sentenced_for_second_time .html.

[4] RLS Staff, "Former Chairwoman of Rutgers University Philosophy Department Sentenced to 12 Years for Raping Disabled Man," January 15, 2016, https://www.rlsmedia.com/article/former-chairwoman-rutgers-university-philosophy-department-sentenced-12-years-raping.

[5] Anna Stubblefield, "Sound and Fury: When Opposition to Facilitated Communication Functions as Hate Speech," *Disability Studies Quarterly* 31, no. 4 (2011), https://dsq-sds.org/article/view/1729/1777.

[6] Daniel Engber, "The Strange Case of Anna Stubblefield," *The New York Times Magazine* (October 20, 2015), https://www.nytimes.com /2015/10/25/magazine/the-strange-case-of-anna-stubblefield.html.

[7] Anna Stubblefield, *"Revealing Whiteness: The Unconscious Habits of Racial Privilege* (review)," *Hypatia* 23, no. 2 (Spring 2008), https://muse.jhu.edu/article/239750.

[8] Daniel Engber, "The Strange Case of Anna Stubblefield," *The New York Times Magazine* (October 20, 2015), https://www.nytimes.com /2015/10/25/magazine/the-strange-case-of-anna-stubblefield.html.

[9] For photos, see http://www.robeprobe.com/vote_details.php?judge _id=1295&user_id=2720&judge_Siobhan_A._Teare ; and https://www. google.com/search?tbm=isch&sxsrf=ALeKk01H-LkcguNfMLZbh68S pYdHHKlkqQ%3A1600040575690&source=hp&biw=1113&bih=714&ei=f65 eX8CnJ6uF9PwPnOWV6Aw&q=Siobhan+Teare&oq=Siobhan+Teare&gs_l cp=CgNpbWcQAzIECAAQGFDbBFjbBGDPCWgAcAB4AIABuQGIAbkBk gEDMC4xmAEAoAECoAEBqgELZ3dzLXdpei1pbWc&sclient=img&ved=0 ahUKEwiA44zRp-frAhWrAp0JHZxyBc0Q4dUD CAY&uact=5#imgrc=o9Us4mzpbTaP6M

[10] Engber, "The Strange Case of Anna Stubblefied," https://www. nytimes.com/2015/10/25/magazine/the-strange-case-of-anna-stubblefield. html.

[11] Ibid.

[12] Daniel, Engber, "What Anna Stubblefield Believed She Was Doing," *New York Times (Online)* (February 3, 2016), http://www. nytimes.com/2016/02/03/magazine/what-anna-stubblefield-believed-she-was-doing.html?partner=bloomberg.

[13] Peter Singer and Jeff McMahan, "Who is the Victim in the Anna Stubblefield Case?," *New York Times (Online)* (April 3, 2017), https://www.nytimes.com/2017/04/03/opinion/who-is-the-victim-in-the-anna-stubblefield-case.html.

For another attempt at defending Stubblefield, see Astra Taylor, "Anna Stubblefield was Convicted of Raping her Disabled Student. But was the Trial Fair?," *Splinter* (November 12, 2015), https://splinternews.com/.com/anna-stubblefield-was-convicted-of-raping-her-disabled-1793852818.

[14] For instance, see Eleanor Gordon-Smith, "What Does the Anna Stubblefield Case Teach Us about Sentencing and Sexual Assault?," June 19, 2017, https://www.abc.net.au/news/2017-06-19/anna-stubblefield-what-matters-in-sentencing-for-sexual-assault/8630074; Eric Schliesser, "On Philosophical Authority (McMahan & Singer on the Stubblefield Case)," April 4, 2017, https://digressionsnimpressions.typepad.com/digressions impressions/2017/04/on-philosophical-authority-mcmahan-singer-on-the-stubblefield-case.html; and Brian Leiter, "Singer and McMahan on the Stubblefield Case," April 3, 2017, https://leiterreports.typepad.com /blog/2017/04/singer-and-mcmahan-on-the-stubblefield-case.html#more.

[15] Cf. Singer's and McMahon's "logic is flawed because it supposes that for someone to be harmed, they have to actually perceive the harm being done to them." Kevin Mintz, "Ableism, Ambiguity, and the Anna Stubblefield Case," *Disability & Society* 32, no. 10 (2017), 1669. The "response [of Stubblefield's supporters] to [the] rape [she committed] is not only misdirected, it is unethical and shameful." Mark Sherry, "Facilitated Communication, Anna Stubblefield and Disability Studies," *Disability & Society* 31, no. 7 (August 17, 2016), 979. "Again, let's be clear on what [Singer and McMahon] are saying: if someone is intellectually disabled enough, then it might be okay to rape them, so long as they don't resist, since a lack of physical struggle justifies an assumption that someone is enjoying being raped." Nathan J. Robinson, "Now Peter Singer Argues that it Might be Okay to Rape Disabled People," *Current Affairs* (April 4, 2017), https://www.currentaffairs.org/2017/04/now-peter-singer-argues-that-it-might-be-okay-to-rape-disabled-people

[16] Paul R. Gross and Norman Levitt, *Higher Superstition* (Baltimore: Johns Hopkins University Press, 1994). Alan D. Sokal and J. Bricmont, *Fashionable Nonsense: Postmodern Intellectuals' Abuse of Science* (New York: Picador, 1998).

[17] Divya Kishore, "2+2=4? New York Professor Says Purity of Math Reeks of 'White Supremacist Patriarchy' and Internet Loses it," August 10, 2020, https://meaww.com/brooklyn-new-york-college-professor-says-purity-math-reeks-of-white-supremacist-patriarchy.

[18] For one example, see Anne Fadiman, The Spirit Catches You and You Fall Down: A Hmong Child, her American Doctors, and the Collision of Two Cultures (New York: Farrar, Straus and Giroux, 1997).

[19] The acceptance of "bears," some obese, some hyper-muscular, some both, among the predominate gay subculture is an important instance of "fat = sexy" in our own time.

[20] https://www.njcourts.gov/attorneys/assets/opinions/appellate/p ublished/a2112-15.pdf.

[21] Daniel Engber, "The Strange Case of Anna Stubblefield, Revisited," *The New York Times Magazine* (April 5, 2018), https://www.nytimes.com/2018/ 04/05/magazine/the-strange-case-of-anna-stubblefield-revisited.html.

[22] Daniel Engber, "What Anna Stubblefield Believed She Was Doing," *New York Times (Online)* (February 3, 2016), https://www.nytimes.com/2016/02/03/magazine/what-anna-stubblefield-believed-she-was-doing.html. See also Bill Wichert, "Convicted Professor's Jailhouse Letter: I Loved Disabled Man," January 24, 2016, https://www.nj.com/essex/2016/01/in_jailhouse_letter_professor_convicte d_of_sex_ass.html.

[23] Daniel Engber, "The Strange Case of Anna Stubblefield, Revisited," *The New York Times Magazine* (April 5, 2018), https://www.nytimes.com/2018/04/05/magazine/the-strange-case-of-anna-stubblefield-revisited.html.

[24] Anna Stubblefield, "Anti-Black Oppression and the Ethical Significance of African American Identity" (PhD diss., Rutgers University, 2000).

# Chapter 4
*Safe Places in University Life Qua Evil*

*Praenotanda*

The Anna Stubblefield case is admittedly unusual. As noted earlier, most of the time female rapists typically go unacknowledged and consequently unpunished, because those in power do not have the will to punish female predators equally. One major stumbling block to the pursuit of justice in these cases is the commitment to emotionally "safe places" for women. When a commitment to maintain safe places for women interferes with the prosecution of female crimes, safe places are unjust. The next few chapters of this book address the evils of safe places in different contexts.

(1) In this chapter, I address only safe places in an *academic* context. I understand that it is natural for humans to want and need safe places. Ideally, *home* is the safe place we should all have and come to love. The rules that obtain in one's home, however, do not obtain in public places, which by definition must be shared with others. Of course, the line between private and public is sometimes blurred. A university professor's office, for instance, is somehow public if the door is open for visitors, but instantaneously becomes private when the door is shut for a confidential conversation. Likewise, a women's shelter is justified in excluding (mostly)

men to maintain a safe place for women who have been abused, battered, and/or abandoned by (mostly) men. AS AN ASIDE: Feminists are fond of fighting amongst themselves as to who counts as a woman. Should women's shelters be allowed to exclude biological males who identify as women?[1] Feminists also typically object to centers primarily intended to help men enduring abuse and trauma from harmful relationships, despite the fact that an increasing number of abuse victims are men.[2] But *if exclusively female places are permitted, exclusively male places should be permitted too. Like the Roman Catholic priesthood.*

(2) I do not necessarily object to trigger warnings in an academic context or anywhere else, for that matter. Whether conservative reactionaries are prepared to admit it or not, trigger warnings play an important role in old fashioned, white culture at its best. A physician and friend of mine, for instance, always prepares her patients for the delivery of an unfortunate diagnosis by asking the question, "Are you sitting down?" She asks that question, even if the patient is sitting down immediately in front of her. In her private life, she uses the same technique when delivering similar kinds of bad news to friends and family. Thus, whenever the words "Are you sitting down?" ominously issue forth from her lips, her adult children know that something horrible has happened.[3]

Because my friend began learning the art of doctoring from her father, who was also an MD, she is the beneficiary of multiple generations of wisdom. Her expertise testifies to the fact that although people from generations passed did not use the expression *trigger warning*, they did in fact have ways to prepare others for the reception of bad news. Such preparation is an important part of living charity. If one were to dig deeper into the everyday behavior of properly-trained, older people, no doubt one would find other vestigial examples of old-fashioned trigger warnings. When such warnings have been hallowed by generations of use, they are laudably retained by us, their often unworthy heirs. Our ancestors, after all, sometimes did know what they were doing.

*When Safe Places are Bad*

Nevertheless, I do object to safe places in an academic context. Whether we want to admit it or not, educators are obliged to teach students the truth about unpleasant and sometimes nauseating parts of history. Who among us was not in an emotionally unsafe place when s/he first learned about the Holocaust? Or about war in general? Sometimes, simple facts that one must come to terms with to grow up of necessity create emotional distress in the soul. Coming to terms with those facts, however, both from our own time and from history, is still mandatory, even if they make us feel bad.

In an academic context, trigger warnings are acceptable when they alert students to the fact that potentially emotionally difficult material will soon be taught. Students, however, should not have the option of getting out of class or not doing the assigned reading, even if they find the material revolting. Unfortunately, that is precisely what a critical mass of university students are trying to do. To make universities emotionally safer, some university students have in effect called for the banning of books like "Chinua Achebe's *Things Fall Apart,* [which] describes racial violence, and...F. Scott Fitzgerald's *The Great Gatsby,* [which] portrays misogyny and physical abuse." [4] No doubt, the Bible and the Qur'an will be next on the chopping block.

*Making the World Safe(r) for the Unqualified*

But what really is going on here? What do safe places have to do with WHITE, FEMALE PRIVILEGE? The fact of the matter is that the itch for safe places in a university context is a consequence of admitting an unequal number of women to universities, many of whom are simply unqualified. The statistics on the gender gap in American higher education are astounding and easily available. [5] In 1982 (i.e., before this author was born) the number of women completing a BA first surpassed that of men; since then, the number of female graduates has consistently risen, such that now the percentage of female graduates is close to 60%. [6] As regards the population at large, the percentage of the American population who are women and have a college degree surpassed that of American men with a college degree in 2014. [7]

Although the question of why our educational system is failing our boys is important, it must be passed over here to address the negative consequences of depriving qualified and competent men their rightful places at university, especially prestigious universities. The ladies have been brought in to displace the male majority, and what have they done? They demand that universities actively censor the very discourses that universities are morally obligated to have, especially as regards rape and abortion. As earlier chapters of this book have stressed, the new and more comprehensive definition of rape codified in most (perhaps all) jurisdictions that compose the US is only legally binding because women want it to be.

*Rape Discourse*

Defining rape is a tricky thing. We all think we know what rape is, but when it comes to crafting its exact legal definition, all manner of controversy follows. A few years ago, such controversy came to the fore in California, where there was widespread debate about whether the legal definition of the consent required to avoid rape should include the word "ongoing" and what such an addition to the law would mean for people. Of course, when a white, male, privileged, Stanford University student was convicted of sexual assault, but not rape, and given a light sentence, all hell broke loose.[8]

Such controversy regarding the exact definition of rape is largely the result of feminist activism, which has produced a legal system characterized by ubiquitous chatter about rape. Rape-discourse is now politically mandatory, as well it should be. Consequently, all politicians, lawyers, and judges should be able to openly discuss the grimy details of what the legal definition of rape should be. But what happens when the women who have been accepted to university and law school in unequal numbers simply cannot discuss those details without being triggered? Such is now the case. As Jeannie Suk Gersen, a professor at Harvard Law School, has noted in *The New Yorker*,

> My experience at Harvard over the past couple of years tells me that the environment for teaching rape law and other subjects involving gender and violence is changing. Students seem more anxious about classroom discussion, and about approaching the law of sexual violence in particular, than they have ever been in my eight years as a law professor. Student organizations representing women's interests now routinely advise students that they should not feel pressured to attend or participate in class sessions that focus on the law of sexual

violence, and which might therefore be traumatic. These organizations also ask criminal-law teachers to warn their classes that the rape-law unit might "trigger" traumatic memories. Individual students often ask teachers not to include the law of rape on exams for fear that the material would cause them to perform less well. One teacher I know was recently asked by a student not to use the word "violate" in class—as in "Does this conduct violate the law?"—because the word was triggering. Some students have even suggested that rape law should not be taught because of its potential to cause distress.

...

What has made everyone so newly nervous about discussing sexual-assault law in the classroom?[9]

The answer is those women who are unfit for law school because of their emotional incontinence. Same goes for the men who are complicit in their own oppression by marketing themselves as feminist allies, often with an eye to sating their lusts. Why are such persons admitted to law school in the first place? Well, it's because of FEMALE PRIVILEGE.

*You're not qualified. So why the fuck are you here?*

No doubt, what I've just said is offensive to a certain demographic of people; I intend it to be. In response, here I play the devil's advocate. The liberal objection to my position would seem to go, as follows: Out of a commitment to equity, inclusion, and compassion, important institutions (including

Ivy League universities) ought to change their corporate culture so that survivors of sexual assault and rape can flourish on university campuses. And a commitment to justice simultaneously requires a legal culture that punishes rape severely. But such punishment requires the very discourse in law schools that creates emotionally unsafe places for rape survivors. In short, feminists want (1) a university culture that is "emotionally safe" because it outlaws rape discourse or makes that discourse optional; and, (2) a political culture in which rape discourse is mandatory. (1) produces people who cannot function in (2), and yet feminists will also acknowledge that university culture is suppose to prepare people for the broader political culture.

*Abortion*

No political issue on university campuses or in the broader culture is as divisive as abortion. Happily, President Trump's improvements to the US Supreme Court will probably result in the overturning of Roe v. Wade. In consequence, the American people will have to rediscover the importance and necessity of working out their disagreements on that issue democratically and at the state level (i.e., without the intervention of unelected ruling elites in Washington, DC). Because of safe places in universities, however, such discourse regarding abortion is often no longer possible. People cannot discuss the issue civilly, because the educational system they've grown up in has not forced them to develop the necessary skills. As a few Google searches reveal, when pro-lifers on university campuses seek to engage in reasoned, civil debate, leftist student groups typically subvert the conditions necessary for discourse, often with the full endorsement of university administration. [10] Here, for instance, is a description of how one such debate was censored at the University of Oxford in 2014:

> But someone was outraged that we dared to discuss this issue at all. A protest group of around 300 people called "What the f**k is 'Abortion Culture'?" appeared on Facebook that promised to "take along some non-destructive but oh so disruptive instruments to help demonstrate to the anti-choicers just what we think of their 'debate'." We were guilty of promoting "really sh*tty anti-choice rhetoric and probs some cissexism." The foul language indicates how sophisticated the protesters were, while the accusation of cissexism had me reaching for my online urban dictionary...

> The university's students' union also issued a statement that took aim at Brendan and me [i.e., the debate's organizers] for being so offensively attached to our God-given genitals: "The Women's Campaign (WomCam) condemn SFL for holding this debate. It is absurd to think we should be listening to two cisgender men debate about what people with uteruses should be doing with their bodies." Next, the Christ Church Junior Common Room (posh talk for "the committee that run [sic] the students' bar") passed a motion asking their college to decline to room the debate. Eventually, the college caved-in on the grounds that, "there was insufficient time between today and tomorrow to address some concerns they had about the meeting." The pro-life society tried to find an alternative venue but everyone else

said "no." I believe that two colleges agreed only to later rescind their invitations. I was sitting in Paddington Station (in a duffel coat and hat!) ready to jump on a train to Oxford at 4:40 p.m. when I was told that the debate was finally, totally called off. I said the same thing my mother says every time the car stalls or the TV goes on the blink: "This is why people vote UKIP."[11]

A few things to note: (1) Despite their assertions to the contrary, the Leftists threatened to use violence, if need be, to silence their opponents. The following words invite scrutiny: "Take along some non-destructive but oh so disruptive instruments to help demonstrate to the anti-choicers just what we think of their 'debate'." What *instruments* exactly did the author of this threat have in mind? Then again, in an age when verbal violence is to be treated as though it were just as unacceptable as physical violence, if the instruments are *disruptive*, why should they not also be construed as *destructive*? (2) Leftists lack basic logic: "It is absurd to think we should be listening to two cisgender men debate about what people with uteruses should be doing with their bodies." There we have a classic example of the ad hominem circumstantial (a.k.a., the ad hominem abusive) logical fallacy.

> *Let's review: Traditional modes of logic are universally binding, young lady, even if the mandatory nature of traditional logic constitutes a form of patriarchal and Eurocentric oppression. The fact that you hate logic and are no good at it, does not make it less binding on us all.*

(3) Perhaps more importantly, Leftist calls for such censorship presuppose and reveal a kind of patronizing patriarchy. Apparently, such debates are unacceptable, because women on campus are too *weak* to endure open debate regarding abortion laws:

> This is why they [i.e., the White Liberal Matriarchs] believe censorship is justified. And this is why they view free speech as a threat rather than a precious opportunity. People, you see, particularly those to whom subordinate identities (from women and non-binary people to disabled and trans-people) have been attributed, are not strong enough, not resilient enough to hear challenging arguments. They are too traumatised, too liable to "triggering," too morally weak, too susceptible to harm...In short, their feelings will be hurt. And so those good campaigning students are silencing debates on their behalf, on behalf of their right not to be upset, offended, or discomfited. After all, their "comfort" is paramount.[12]

It goes without saying that women (and men too) who are too emotionally incontinent to endure an open debate about the details of abortion law should be expelled from university entirely, because they pose a threat to the very discourse that universities are morally obligated to have.

Regardless, now that third-trimester abortions may very well be made illegal in most of the US, the WLM will have to learn to remain present and to fight fairly about abortion law with their opponents, or be rendered politically impotent.[13] Pro-choice violence is sure to follow when whiny activists fail to achieve their goals through peaceful, democratic means.[14]

> *The pro-life movement was always destined to win, because prolifers were always more committed, more industrious, and more representative of the American people at large. Say what you want, voting at the state level is the only democratic way to deal with this issue.*

## The Election of Donald Trump

The liberal response to the election of Donald Trump in 2016 also illustrates how the commitment to safe places in a university context censors the very discourse that universities are morally obligated to have. In the name of creating emotionally safe places for minorities of various kinds Trump supporters were not allowed to openly reveal that they voted for Trump, nor are they allowed to reveal *why* they voted for him. In consequence, we were left with a political and academic culture in which American citizens were not allowed to openly discuss why the President of the United States was in fact the President of the United States. And no, racism was not one of the more important reasons for Trump's victory, neither was sexism.

Censoring such political discourse created a shitstorm for the mainstream media. Because those who voted for Trump were not allowed to openly reveal that fact, the polling that the mainstream media and government relied upon did not work. Thus, by creating a culture of fear in which Trump supporters were not allowed to reveal whom they voted for without suffering political and/or professional retaliation, the mainstream media rendered themselves useless, and subverted their own job security.

*If your polling is that inaccurate, why the fuck*
*should anyone pay you to conduct polls? If you*
*predicted that Clinton would win by a landslide*
*in 2016, why the fuck should anyone take you*
*seriously now?*

Polling in the 2020 election cycle was likewise untrustworthy. A surprising number of minorities voted for Trump the second time, far more than any mainstream source predicted. Polls were more reliable if responders could respond anonymously. *Newsweek*, for instance, reported that 45% of American men who identified as queer preferred Trump to Biden. [15] That percentage was probably higher, however, because, as already noted, mainstream polling is biased against conservatives. As a gay man myself who fell in that 45%, I do hope for a radical change in terms of permitted discourse. If permitting an open conversation about the pros and cons of Trump with people who reluctantly favored him, as I did, creates unsafe environments for the emotionally incontinent, fuck them. That discourse should be academically mandatory, even if it makes some people feel unsafe.

*No, the discourse that should be mandatory at*
*this institution will not threaten your life. And*
*no, Trump wasn't president because of racism. If*
*you can't civilly discuss the outcome of the*
*election, you lack the emotional maturity that*
*should be universally required for university life.*
*Get the fuck out.*

*Grade Inflation*

Finally, grade inflation has been a problem at universities for quite some time. Harvard is a frequent offender.[16] The arguments surrounding it make people feel uncomfortable, for they require that someone offer an explanation as to what grades are for, and to acknowledge that all people do not have equal abilities. "Modern man,"[17] let us remember, refuses to acknowledge both teleology and the natural inequalities that ever mark the human race despite liberal attempts to make them disappear. The refusal to address the question of what things are for, however, permanently thwarts the natural desire to understand that makes us human. Likewise, the refusal to acknowledge inherent inequalities between people necessarily threatens the good of professionalism, which is mandatory if institutions, including governments and universities, are to function.

Consequently and unsurprisingly, in the midst of objections to grade inflation at Harvard, students rightly posed the question of "whether grades should signify competence or comparison," but did not attempt an answer. Instead, they argued that one should not assume that grade inflation was the primary cause of the frequency of high grades at Harvard. Their tone also revealed their view that grade inflation was not a problem that needed to be addressed.[18] In 2001, Harry Lewis, then Dean of Harvard College, attempted to deflect blame for the situation by pointing out that undergraduate grades had on average steadily risen since at least 1920, and probably since the 1890s. Already in 1894, for instance, "a special...'Committee on Raising the Standard' rued that 'in the present practice Grades A and B are sometimes given too readily,—Grade A for work of not very high merit, and Grade B for work not far above mediocrity.'"[19]

Grade inflation surely has multiple causes. Sloth among undergraduates predisposing them to take courses that are not particularly challenging is one, unfortunate cause. A professional, political, and intellectual culture in which high grades on paper are more valued than intellectual curiosity and academic risk-taking is another. Nonetheless, the desire to create emotionally safe places for the unqualified is surely one cause of grade inflation. The situation has been aptly described by two academics who professionally study trends in higher education, as follows:

> Every generation of college students has much in common with its immediate predecessors, but each generation is also different. According to deans of students, current undergraduates are more coddled, protected, and spoiled than previous students. They told us, "This is a generation that has never been allowed to skin their knees." "They all won awards at everything they ever tried—most improved player, fourth runner-up, best seven-year-old speller born on March 8." Their parents are the "helicopter parents" whose children were "never permitted to fail" at any undertaking. They grew up with an inflated sense of accomplishment and expect to continue to receive awards or at least praise for everything they do.

> Interviews with two dozen employers produced a similar response. They criticized the recent college grads they hired for "expecting to be rewarded for showing up," "wanting the keys to the kingdom on day one," "asking for a raise

after a month of mediocre work," "having their parents fight their battles," and "being unable to take criticism."

Here's the problem. Three out of five undergraduates now believe their inflated grades understate their true academic ability. To put this into perspective, 45 percent are coming to college weak in basic skills, having to take at least one remedial course in math or writing. Over the years that number has risen almost as quickly as their grades. On top of this, current undergraduates find the courses they are taking quite challenging. Fewer than one in ten (7 percent) describe them as easy, and more than half (54 percent) say they are difficult or very difficult.[20]

Clearly, to accommodate such coddled students (i.e., customers) and to create the emotionally safe places they have to have in order to feel a certain way, standards must be reduced. As a result, grades continue to mean less and less and what grades are for is no longer clear. But if grades are not an honest and transparent reflection of anything in particular, the universities that give them will soon no longer be able to justify their own existence.

Two anecdotes from my own life shed light on the problem: (1) The first is how grades from mainstream institutions are treated by at least one academically rigorous school on the margins that still has a high reputation in mainstream academia. A friend of mine who was president of the student body at Deep Springs College, assures me that when the application materials of applicants are reviewed there, grades are sometimes disregarded entirely. After all, bad grades are often the result of bright students coming into conflict with stupid, incompetent, and/or prejudiced teachers, who feel threatened when the excellence of a smarter person in the classroom is openly manifested. Those with failing grades from elsewhere, however, often prove themselves to be excellent students when they no longer have to deal with teachers, parents, fellow students, and/or administrators who are dipshits.

(2) An acquaintance at a major American university who is now approaching the end of his career has explained to me what happens at his institution when a tenure-track position in the humanities opens up. An untold number of applications from seemingly qualified candidates piles up almost immediately. The search committee first opens candidates' transcripts only to find that almost everyone has straight As. Next, the committee reads the letters of recommendation, but these too reveal nothing substantial about the candidates, because each letter is absolutely glowing. Apparently, each letter is crafted to make the search committee feel that the candidate under consideration is not merely the best among those being considered, but the best candidate that there can ever be. As such, grades and letters of recommendation can no longer be trusted to give a reasonable assessment of a candidate's qualifications and abilities, because identical grades do not allow people's abilities to be differentiated, and the letters are patently dishonest.

In the case of one tenure-track position that was recently filled, the search committee received word from administration that they were obligated to disregarded every male candidate, solely because an insufficient number of women taught in the department in question; which is to say, the careers of the male candidates, regardless of their merits, were sacrificed on the altar of affirmative action. In the end, the woman offered the position was the only female applicant whose research interests fit the needs and mission of the department. Thus, she passed liberal scrutiny solely because of her gender, and conservative scrutiny because of her academic interests. The situation is a shame, however, because the woman they hired actually has the qualifications necessary to compete with men without being coddled because of her gender. Nonetheless, because her gender was the most important factor in the search committee's decision, she cannot be said to have *earned* what she currently enjoys.

*Tacky. Liberal. Incoherent*

The liberal commitment to "inclusion" (i.e. to unjustly admitting to university the unprepared and far more women than men) requires the admission of the emotionally incontinent and emotionally unqualified. And because we are discussing prestigious institutions with a limited number of seats, the inclusion of emotionally unqualified women requires depriving qualified male candidates of what is rightfully theirs. In place of such "inclusion," I propose instead a commitment to professionalism. Professionalism, however, requires the exclusion of those who lack talent, training, and skill. Those who cannot discuss the grimy details of rape, the election of 2016, and abortion, and those who require emotionally safe places in order to function, both among faculty and students, should consequently be expelled. Same goes for those who cannot help but faint at the sight of blood in medical schools. If you cannot do the work required by the position, you are not qualified. And the reasons why you cannot do the work do not matter.

*You've judged me unworthy of the Ivy League. Well, now that judgment is mutual.*

**CHAPTER 4 NOTES**

[1] Amy Eileen Hamm, "After Losing City Grant, Vancouver Rape Relief Say They Have No Plans to Scale Back Services or Public Education," *Feminist Current* (March 5, 2020), https://www.feministcurrent .com/2020/03/05/after-losing-city-grant-vancouver-rape-relief-say-they-have-no-plans-to-scale-back-services-public-education/.

[2] For mainstream, feminist opposition to the Canadian Centre for Men and Families, whose first hub opened in Toronto in 2014, see Alex Nino Gheciu, "Controversial Men's Rights Group Fundraising for a Centre for Men and Families," *The Star* (August 15, 2013), https://www.thestar.com/news/gta/2013/08/15/controversial_mens_rights _group_fundraising_for_a_centre_for_men_and_families.html; and Mike Donachie, "Controversial Men's Equality Group Wants to Turn a Corner with Toronto Centre," *Metro* (November 20, 2014), https://web.archive.org/web/20150531133245/http://metronews.ca/news/to ronto/1217473/controversial-mens-equality-group-wants-to-turn-a-corner-with-toronto-centre/.

[3] Note that in my native dialect, the expression "to be floored" refers to being so shocked at the first hearing of bad news that one (almost?) falls to the floor. (For instance, "When Hilary Clinton heard the news that Trump won the election, she was floored.") Thus, the question "Are you sitting down?" serves to prevent the one hearing bad news from being literally *floored.*

[4] Greg Lukianoff and Jonathan Haidt, "The Coddling of the American Mind," *The Atlantic* (September 2015), https://www.theatlantic. com/magazine/archive/2015/09/the-coddling-of-the-american-mind /399356/.

[5] For the official statistics, see https://www.statista.com/statistics /185157/number-of-bachelor-degrees-by-gender-since-1950/ and https:// www.theatlantic.com /business/archive/2017/11/gender-education-gap/546 677/. For commentary on such inequalities, see, for instance, Alana Semuels, "Poor Girls are Leaving their Brothers Behind," *The Atlantic* (November 27, 2017), https://www.theatlantic.com/business/archive/2017/ 11/gender-education-gap/546677/; Daniel Borzelleca, "The Male-Female Ratio in College," *Forbes* (February 16, 2012), https://www.forbes.com /sites/ccap/2012/02/16/the-male-female-ratio-in-college/#7a4de0e0fa52; and "In a First, Women Surpass Men in College Degrees," *CBS NEWS* (April 26, 2011), https://www.cbsnews.com/news/in-a-first-women-surpass-men-in-college-degrees/.

[6] https://www.statista.com/statistics/185157/number-of-bachelor-degrees-by-gender-since-1950/.

[7] https://www.statista.com/statistics/184272/educational-attainment-of-college-diploma-or-higher-by-gender/. See also https:// dailycaller.com/2021/10/20/stone-young-men-avoiding-college-better-options/.

[8] For some examples from the mainstream media regarding the legal definition of rape in California and its application, see Bill Chappell, "California Enacts 'Yes Means Yes' Law, Defining Sexual Consent," *NPR* (September 29, 2014), https://www.npr.org/sections/thetwo-way/2014/09/29/352482932/california-enacts-yes-means-yes-law-defining-sexual-consent; Emanuella Grinberg, "Schools Preach 'Enthusiastic' Yes in Sex Consent Education," *CNN* (September 29, 2014), https://www.cnn.com/2014/09/03/living/affirmative-consent-school-policy/index.html; Dayna Evans, "Why Brock Turner Wasn't Technically Convicted of Rape, *The CUT* (June 7, 2016), https://www.thecut.com/2016/06/brock-turner-sexual-assault-felony.html; Kirsten Salyer, "Why We Can't Call Brock Turner a 'Rapist'," *TIME* (June 9, 2016), https://time.com/4362949/stanford-sexual-assault-not-rape/; Christina Garcia, "Assemblymember: California's Definition of 'Rape' Must Change," *TIME* (June 15, 2016), https://time.com/4369095/californias-definition-of-rape/; and Bridgette Dunlap, "How California's New Rape Law Could Be a Step Backward," *RollingStone* (September 1, 2016), https://www.rollingstone.com/culture/culture-news/how-californias-new-rape-law-could-be-a-step-backward-250347/.

[9] Jeannie Suk Gersen, "The Trouble with Teaching Rape Law," *The New Yorker* (December 15, 2014), https://www.newyorker.com/news/news-desk/trouble-teaching-rape-law.

[10] For some examples, see Matthew Davies and Adam Dayan, "Abortion Debate Cancelled," *The Oxford Student* (November 20, 2014), https://www.oxfordstudent.com/2014/11/20/abortion-debate-cancelled/; Tim Black, "Oxford, Abortion and the Closing of the Western Mind," *spiked* (February 2, 2015), https://www.spiked-online.com/2015/02/02/oxford-abortion-and-the-closing-of-the-western-mind/; and Brett Bundale, "How University Campuses Became Ground Zero for Canada's Abortion Debate," *CBC NEWS* (September 9, 2018), https://www.cbc.ca/news/canada/nova-scotia/abortion-debate-at-canada-s-universities-critics-1.4816333.

[11] Tim Stanley, "Oxford Students Shut Down Abortion Debate: Free Speech Is under Assault on Campus," *The Telegraph Online* (November 19, 2014), https://www.telegraph.co.uk/news/politics/11239437/Oxford-students-shut-down-abortion-debate.-Free-speech-is-under-assault-on-campus.html.

[12] Black, "Oxford, Abortion and the Closing of the Western Mind," *spiked* (February 2, 2015), https://www.spiked-online.com/2015/02/02/oxford-abortion-and-the-closing-of-the-western-mind/. Note that the ellipsis appears in the original.

[13] To be fair, certain, insightful liberals have known for a few years now that Roe v. Wade was destined to be overturned. For one's reassessment of the issue giving both sides equal weight, see Caitlin Flanagan, "The Dishonesty of the Abortion Debate: Why We Need to Face the Best

Arguments from the Other Side," *The Atlantic* (December 2019), https://www.theatlantic.com/magazine/archive/2019/12/the-things-we-cant-face/600769/.

¹⁴ Such pro-choice violence has now come to Poland. For more on this, see Vanessa Gera, "Poles Protest Abortion Ban in Church and on Streets," *Associated Press News* (October 25, 2020), https://apnews.com/article/womens-rights-poland-europe-warsaw-0e63ff083f4a8efa3a98abab5e0fd6f9.

¹⁵ For two mainstream responses to the unreliability of polling in the 2020 election, see Ryan Cooper, "How Progressives Should Respond to Another Polling Failure," *The Week* (November 5, 2020), https://theweek.com/articles/948105/how-progressives-should-respond-another-polling-failure; and David Faris, "Was Trump Ever As Unpopular As We Thought?" *The Week* (November 12, 2020), https://theweek.com/articles/948463/trump-ever-unpopular-thought.

¹⁶For a glimpse into the history of grade inflation at the American university with the most exaggerated reputation, see Harry R. Lewis, "The Racial Theory of Grade Inflation," *The Harvard Crimson* (April 23, 2001), https://www.thecrimson.com/article/2001/4/23/the-racial-theory-of-grade-inflation/; Kate L. Rakoczy, "Faculty Agree Grade Inflation Troubling," *The Harvard Crimson* (November 21, 2001), https://www.thecrimson.com/article/2001/11/21/faculty-agree-grade-inflation-troubling-after/; Brittney L. Moraski, "Report: Grade Inflation Persists: As and A-minuses Comprise Half of Grades Awarded in '05–'06," *The Harvard Crimson* (May 9, 2007), https://www.thecrimson.com/article/2007/5/9/report-grade-inflation-persists-over-half/; Matthew Q. Clarida and Nicholas P. Fandos, "Substantiating Fears of Grade Inflation, Dean Says Median Grade at Harvard College Is A-, Most Common Grade Is A," *The Harvard Crimson* (December 3, 2013), https://www.thecrimson.com/article/2013/12/3/grade-inflation-mode-a/; The Crimson Staff, "The A's Have It," *The Harvard Crimson* (December 4, 2013), https://www.thecrimson.com/article/2013/12/4/grade-inflation-harvard/; and Arthur Levine and Diane Dean, "Why Grade Inflation (Even at Harvard) Is a Big Problem," *The Washington Post* (December 20, 2013), https://www.washingtonpost.com/news/answer-sheet/wp/2013/12/20/why-grade-inflation-even-at-harvard-is-a-big-problem/.

¹⁷ I put the term in scare quotes because the term has never included sound-minded people like me born after 1980.

¹⁸ Staff, "The A's Have It," https://www.thecrimson.com/article/2013/12/4/grade-inflation-harvard/.

¹⁹ Lewis, "The Racial Theory of Grade Inflation," https://www.thecrimson.com/article/2001/4/23/the-racial-theory-of-grade-inflation/.

²⁰ Levine and Dean, "Why Grade Inflation (Even at Harvard) Is a Big Problem," *The Washington Post*, https://www.washingtonpost.com

/news/answer-sheet/wp/2013/12/20/why-grade-inflation-even-at-harvard-is-a-big-problem/.

# Chapter 5

*Safe Places Elsewhere: Anecdotal Evidence*

A commitment to safe places in non-academic contexts likewise often results in thoroughgoing incoherence and standards that are far more demanding for men than for women. Here, I rehearse some anecdotal evidence from my own life testifying to WHITE FEMALE PRIVILEGE, and to how "safe places" for women are sometimes simply unjust in real life.

## *Incompetence in the Workplace*

One summer I volunteered nearly full-time for a politician I honestly liked, with a track record I could support. He proved himself unfit for office, however, by keeping on his campaign one woman who was particularly incompetent: Despite her best efforts, she simply could not learn how to attach a file to an email, and yet her position required basic computer skills. Were it not for her gender, she would certainly have been fired. Firing her, however, would have made someone's granny cry, and with a commitment to safe places we can't have that. From what I can tell, we lost the campaign because the man running for office refused to fire volunteers like her. No doubt, she was truly doing her best, but that doesn't matter, because the best she could do was not good enough.

*Lack of Basic Hygiene*

At another point in my life, I was renting a room in a large house with six other people while going to graduate school. One of the housemates was a six-hundred-pound (mostly) white woman named Kimberly who identified as Native American and failed (refused?) to practice basic hygiene. She habitually left her vaginal flow on the toilet seat for other people to clean up. I will never forget once running to the bathroom to take a shit and sitting in her unhygienic mess because there was no time to wipe down the seat beforehand. My other housemates in private acknowledged that Kimberly's lack of cleanliness was a problem, but when it came to holding her accountable at a house meeting, we were all too cowardly to say anything.

My experience dealing with group cowardice and a woman's vaginal flow revealed to me an intriguing (and viscerally repulsive) facet of (mostly) WHITE FEMALE PRIVILEGE. The patriarchal mores we have received from our ancestors, dictate that it is always wrong to cause a woman embarrassment, and especially shame, for anything she might do during or because of menses. Objecting to a woman's misconduct when she bleeds, after all, creates an emotionally unsafe place for her; under the old patriarchy causing such shame was always bad form. But to explore this matter a bit more deeply, an important question keeps asserting itself: Is woman man's equal? Do women actually want to be held to the same standards as men? Even when suffering the monthly curse? If fourth-wave feminists are serious when it comes to denying all gender-essentialism, they must accept that when women do bad things during and/or because of menstruation, the due consequences for their misconduct should not be reduced because they bleed. In Kimberly's case, that means having no qualms about openly confronting her about her lack of hygiene and, if she refuses to reform herself, kicking her out of the house. If kicking her out means homelessness, then so be it. If men failed or refused to clean up their misplaced bodily fluids in the bathroom, I would, of course, hold them to the same, punitive standard.

*Screaming in the Doctor's Office*

Finally, the physician I referred to in the last chapter who is good with trigger warnings, has had her difficulties with her patients. She's an OB-GYN by training, so all of her patients were once women. Because she completed medical school before 1982 (i.e., before the system was prejudiced in favor of female applicants), one knows she actually earned it. Rumor has it that she is such an excellent diagnostician that her male colleagues were actually afraid to disagree with her. As she once pointed out to me with a smirk, "If you want to know what's wrong with someone's vagina, it helps to have one yourself." Let's call her Dr. Mary.

Dr. Mary is now retired. The art of doctoring, as she has often pointed out to me, sometimes imposes upon the physician the moral and professional obligation to deliver accurate and unfortunate diagnoses to one's patients. That's just a more formal way of saying that doctors, like priests, are required on occasion to speak the truth that harms. The truth sometimes harms, but the harm involved does not detract from the obligation to declare the truth, for truth is binding, even when it makes us feel bad.

Sometimes delivering an accurate and unfortunate diagnosis goes as well as it can. Dr. Mary, for instance, once had to tell an 80-year-old, black church lady that she had contracted a venereal disease. (I obviously don't know the patient's name, but let's call her Ms. Alma Johnson.) Upon hearing the bad news, Alma remarked, "Well, doctor, how'd I get that?" To which the doctor said, "Well, Ms. Johnson, that's an excellent question. How did you get that?" Response: "Well, I guess I be doin' what I ain't suppose to be doin'!" And the doctor said, "Well, I guess you be right." In the conversation that followed, Ms. Johnson confessed that she had fornicated with a cute 50-year-old she met at church. Importantly, her respectful response and gratitude for the doctor's accurate diagnosis revealed that Alma knew that her venereal disease was God's just punishment for her sins of the flesh. I have no doubt that she repented. Upon reflection, one sees that her fate was not so horrible; if one is going to contract a venereal disease, one's 80s is the best season of life in which to do so.

*Just because you met that cute 50-year-old at church does not mean that he can't give you gonorrhea. O no, it does not!*

One can only imagine my disgust and shock when Dr. Mary told me that sometimes patients would respond to her unfortunate, but accurate diagnoses with the grossest forms of verbal abuse. By "grossest forms of verbal abuse," I mean that some have screamed and called her a "bitchy cunt," precisely because she delivered an accurate diagnosis. This would happen on average once every two weeks. When one adds it all up, over the course of twenty-five years in gynecology, that amounts to 600 women screaming in the doctor's office, because the doctor did her duty to deliver accurate diagnoses. Naturally, because of WHITE FEMALE PRIVILEGE the patients involved suffered no negative consequences whatsoever for their verbal violence. Not one of the 600 ever bothered to apologize afterwards for causing her such degradation. After twenty-five years in private practice, Dr. Mary got the hell out of gynecology and spent the rest of her career working for the military, where the disrespectful, insubordinate, and/or verbally abusive receive the punishment they deserve.

*Equality?*

When Dr. Mary's patients got to screaming, what really were they doing? What (false) beliefs are presupposed by their misconduct? The error of those raving maenads is a quintessentially American one: an erroneous belief in equality where in fact there is none. In this case, the Americanist error plays itself out, as follows: The doctor has caused the patient psychological pain; therefore, the patient is justified in retaliating by causing the doctor a comparable amount of pain. Such behavior would be a bit more understandable if patient and doctor were equals, but in fact they're not. Because the patient-doctor relationship is not one between equals, but between superior and inferior, no such equality obtains. Which is to say, when professionally called upon to do so, the doctor is justified in causing the patient the harm that inevitably arises from the delivery of an accurate, but unfortunate diagnosis, and the patient is not (and should not) be permitted to retaliate, because a patient is not her doctor's equal.

> *She has the right to hurt you; and you don't (and shouldn't) have the right to hurt her back in retaliation. Bitch, please. Mind your place.*

*Verbal Violence = Physical Violence?*

The misconduct of Dr. Mary's patients goes deeper, however, and requires further analysis. Liberals are fond of asserting that "verbal violence is just as bad as physical violence." They do so to justify their demands that those in power censure and silence conservative speech in government, universities, and the media. Once one takes a step back from their desire to deprive their opponents of their right to free speech, however, the liberal claim at issue is an interesting one deserving of serious consideration by ethicists (and by the rest of us too). Is it actually the case that *verbal* violence is *just* as bad as physical violence? What happens if one answers that question in the affirmative? Without working through all the pros and cons of that intriguing question, for the sake of argument, here I hypothetically agree with the libs. Verbal violence *is* just as bad as physical violence. I will now apply that general, hypothetical position to the scenario at hand.

The first question required by our hypothesis would be whether the behavior of Dr. Mary's patients constitutes verbal violence. No doubt my liberal critics would dispute my claim, but the fact is that yes, screaming at your gynecologist and calling her a "bitchy cunt," because she has done her duty to give you an accurate diagnosis, does constitute verbal violence. But if (A) the patients in our scenario are guilty of verbal violence, and (B) verbal violence (in women) is just as bad as physical violence (in men), the guilt of Dr. Mary's patients equals that of physically violent men. So, now we're in a real feminist pickle, because in that case, screaming, female patients are just as despicable, and just as deserving of punishment, as violent men (e.g., men who beat their wives). Feminist discourse, however, going back to the 1950s, has always presupposed that men are essentially more violent than women, and that men ought to be punished severely for their violence. Given the gender essentialism presupposed by such discourse, because men are (supposedly) by nature more prone to violence than women, the number of men and women punished for such violence should not be equal.

*Man violent; Woman always the abused victim?*

Such feminist essentialism, however, cannot endure scrutiny, if, as my liberal interlocutors claim, verbal violence (including the verbal violence of women) really is *just* as bad as physical violence (including domestic violence for which men before 1960 are now justly notorious).

In short, *if* verbal violence is *just* as bad as physical violence, the following necessarily follows: If a woman does scream at her doctor and calls her a "bitchy cunt" in response to an accurate diagnosis, the patient is guilty of grave misconduct. Due punishment for such misconduct (and sin) should include enduring the public shaming of being openly compared to a man who beats his wife. And if the screaming patient is herself a victim of domestic violence, the rest of us are justified in openly concluding that she's just as despicable as the man who beat her.

*The only "bitchy cunt" in this scenario, is **you,** when **you** will not stop screaming.*

*Violent Urges*

No doubt, my opponents will react violently to my simple observation that yes, some abused women really are just as bad as the men who abuse them, if they're just as violent. The same opponents would probably find some excuse to explain why screaming women are somehow not responsible for their acts when they scream. Nonetheless, despite such special pleading to the contrary, the fact of their guilt remains, and that guilt requires additional scrutiny. Besides revealing their belief in an equality that does not in fact exist, when Dr. Mary's patients got to screaming, what exactly were they doing?

Although many answers can be given to that question, at some basic level Dr. Mary's patients were failing to control their urges. The objects of urges vary, but every urge qua urge is the same. My opponents will, no doubt, claim that because Dr. Mary's patients were suffering urges they supposedly could not control, that they're somehow not guilty of engaging in uncalled-for verbal violence. They may, perhaps, be *responsible* for their acts, but they're not *guilty* of anything that merits punishment, or so my opponents might argue. Is it the case that someone's guilt is reduced if s/he supposedly cannot act otherwise because of an urge?

The answer to that question is no. And given the canons of punitive justice demanded by feminists in the face of male violence, they must accept that even if the screaming ladies in the doctor's office are suffering uncontrollable urges, that they're still guilty (and not merely responsible), and their guilt still merits punishment. Let's see how such ethical reasoning plays out in the paradigmatic case of male on female rape. Here, I argue disjunctively: When a man rapes a woman it is either the case that (A) he could have done otherwise or (B) not. If (A), we should all agree that he is guilty of grave misconduct and ought to be punished. But what about (B)? What if it is the case that at least sometimes when men rape women, they simply *cannot* do otherwise? If we could know for certain that the male rapist in question actually was powerless over his urges, how should we respond to his misconduct?

Regardless of how we should respond, the historic feminist response to male-on-female rape is that even if such men literally cannot control their urges, they should still be punished. And a single act of rape merits lifelong punishments. One point of such punishment is to inject fear into the broader culture so that other men in moments of temptation will actually control their dicks, abstain from rape, and (perhaps) avoid burning in hell forever for their violence and lusts. In short, the point of such punishments is to regulate male conduct through *fear.*

*Fear = good.*
*Lack of fear = bad.*

But if unacceptable behavior in men ought to be minimized by fear, unacceptable behavior in women should likewise be regulated by fear. For feminism has declared all of us equal.

*It doesn't matter if you did it only once.*
*You're still guilty.*
*Your Behavior has Consequences.*
*Because you're Human.*

Socially, Dr. Mary's patients deserve shame from the rest of us as due punishment for their behavior. But what should the political consequences be for their misconduct? Although all citizens should be offered healthcare, healthcare is not so basic a right that it can never be taken away. In this, healthcare is like housing, education, or freedom. Such things should be offered to all citizens, but sometimes they should be taken away as due punishment for particularly severe forms of misconduct. Young people who are particularly violent, for instance, should be expelled from high school, if their violence interferes with the reasonable (and laudable) aspirations of their classmates to learn. Likewise, people, like Kimberly, who expect others (including me) to clean up their viscerally repulsive mess, should be denied housing, if their lack of basic hygiene threatens humane living conditions for other people. As regards Dr. Mary's abusive patients, if they are not prepared to apologize for their verbal violence and to reform themselves, they should be denied healthcare in the future, even in emergencies. Because no one has an inviolable right to anyone else's labor, no medical professional should be forced to risk the degradation of treating them. Instead, let those bitches die. Bitch, please. Mind your place.

*Safe Places = Bad*

Of course, the claims I've made in this chapter regarding verbal violence would never be permitted in mainstream contexts. Openly airing such arguments, after all, would create emotionally unsafe places for women who, when push comes to shove, refuse to accept their guilt, even though the rest of us already know that they're guilty. Nevertheless, if feminism is allowed to bring male wickedness to the fore and demand that it be punished, masculinism should be allowed to do the same to female wickedness. Without the freedom to hold women accountable for their misconduct by denying them an emotionally safe place, we don't have equality; we have WHITE FEMALE PRIVILEGE.

# Chapter 6

*Safe Places in Public: Tacky, Liberal, Incoherent*

In case anecdotal evidence from my own life fails to persuade people that injustice sometimes results from a commitment to maintain emotionally safe places for white women in everyday life, here I rehearse other, quintessentially liberal forms of incoherence that arise from safe places when they simply do not work or are prima facie absurd. (Note that *sometimes* is the key word in sentence immediately preceding. As noted earlier, at other times justice requires maintaining emotionally safe places for women, especially at home. Maintaining a safe home for one's wife is arguably a Christian man's chief duty towards her.) Naturally, liberal policy in the end proves incoherent, because an emotionally safe place for one group creates emotional distress for another, unnecessarily wastes large sums of money, or both.

*Racist Tears*

We begin with emotionally safe places for some women, but not for all. A persistent complaint among black women is that when white women cannot function in the work place, they just start crying and the world immediately capitulates to their demands. White women's tears are powerful and bolster a white woman's status qua delicate and helpless victim, but deprive black women (and others too) of the equality required by justice at work. As one black woman has described the situation in general,

> Perhaps the only thing deadlier to a Black person's soul and well-being than actually being killed or incarcerated are the tears of a white woman—among other weaponized emotions. White women's emotions, particularly their tears, have taken countless lives over the generations. These tears and emotions are weapons of mass destruction and we rarely allows [sic] ourselves the chance to have an honest conversation about it. White women tears kill the soul, they make you doubt yourself and your right to exist, they render you voiceless because an emotionally distraught white woman becomes the priority in whatever space she is in. It doesn't matter if you are right—once her tears are activated, you cease to exist. And few things bring other white people—especially men, and sometimes no matter how misogynist they are—to a white woman's defense than her declaring that she is feeling hurt, sad, or discomfited by the words, arguments or actions (no matter how reasonable or nonviolent) of a Black person. Jobs have been lost, friendships ended, and sometimes those tears can send the wrong person to jail. White woman tears are not simply a release; they are a tool.[1]

To get a sense of one particularly egregious individual example, consider this comment on a different blog post dedicated to the same theme:

> Two years ago, I was barked on by a [bipolar] white woman at my job. I barked right back on her. She ran crying to a supervisor. Somehow I was called to meet with the only Black supervisor at my job. That heifer had the nerve to DEFEND the white woman's tears. I no longer give a single f**k about any of their feelings. I call things as they are and keep it moving. They are not the end all and be all of my existence.[2]

Surely, we can all see that emotionally safe places for the white women described in these and similar reports perpetuate the oppression of blacks. Black women demand the freedom to speak the truth that harms, and white women respond with verbal violence because of their emotional incontinence. Although I cannot fathom the degradation that most American blacks have endured, I too am fed up with the misconduct of those white, privileged cunts and wish to be an ally.

*Hunting in the US*

Hunting seems to cause a critical mass of people emotional troubles; hunting is not thereby made less necessary for the common good, however. In the US, deer hunting is the most controversial form, despite the fact that responsible deer hunting is the only financially responsible way to keep the cervine population under control and provides the poor with a healthy and delicious form of animal protein, which is often lacking in their diet.[3] Besides the joys of eating venison, humans benefit from deer hunting by the reduction in auto accidents caused thereby. Without hunting, the number of auto accidents skyrockets and the deer that do not die in those accidents typically starve to death.

And yet, the White Liberal Matriarchy simply cannot stand the thought of conservative meanies with guns killing Bambi's mom and eating her flesh. So far, the WLM has devised two, alternative means of keeping the cervine population under control: Insert all the deer with contraceptive darts or perform invasive surgeries to render them sterile. Only when one realizes that contraceptives for deer in the state of Connecticut alone would cost tax payers $135 million every two years, does one realize the lunacy that results from the liberal aversion to hunting.[4] As regards deer vasectomies, Staten Island's deer sterilization program cost taxpayers $4.1 million. The money, apparently, was not properly spent.[5] The city of Ann Arbor, MI, (fondly derided by Michiganders as "The People's Republic of Ann Arbor: Thirty Square Miles Surrounded by Reality") is likewise so adverse to deer hunting that by November 2018 city government had spent $555,887 on deer sterilization and voted to waste another $182,000 for the same purpose.[6] The Republican-led State Legislature and Republican Governor Rick Snyder, however, had had enough of this bullshit that they forbade such government expenditures in 2019.[7]

Apparently, Ann Arbor hippies feel that the deer are as interested in free love and contraceptive sex as they are. Well, bring in an animal psychic to prove me wrong, but the fact is that no, the deer are not interested in sodomy. Sterilizing them against their will violates their bodily autonomy. And no, there were no deer at Woodstock.

*Deer hunting = cool. Deer contraceptives = bad.*

Despite such idiocy, one can unfortunately, but reasonably infer that financially irresponsible attempts to limit the cervine population will occasionally rear their ugly heads in the future. Because the thought of deer hunting makes devout members of the WLM cry and puts them in emotionally unsafe places, clearly deer hunting ought to be illegal.

*Fuck your activism, bitch. We can't afford yo' shit no more.*

## Hunting in Canada

The most controversial form of hunting in Canada is the hunting of baby seal. Although Canada does not have the same race problems as the US, Canadians have done their duty to accept white guilt when it comes to the European treatment of the First Nations (i.e., "Native Americans" in current American English). Conditions for the First Nations are improving and consequently the various tribes are rediscovering and codifying important parts of their own cultures, including their cuisine. The hunting of animals, including seal and rabbits, and eating their fleshmeats constitute an important part of First Nations' way of life. The Inuit, for instance, rely upon seal hunting to eat, to make a living, and to perpetuate their culture, and it balances the ecosystem. Without hunting, the seal population explodes and threatens the fish population. As the traditional lifestyle of the First Peoples shows us, humans are not suppose to live *apart from* the ecosystem; properly speaking, we're *a part of* the ecosystem. Because we're *a part of*, we have a role to play in keeping the ecosystem balanced precisely by hunting. But what happens when the White Liberal Matriarchy feels that the slaughter of such cute, innocent animals is violent and inhumane, and consequently ought to be illegal?

More specifically, consider the following online petition in opposition to the First Nations enjoying and spreading their own cuisine, and benefiting financially therefrom:

> It was recently announced in an article by Food and Wine, written by David Landsel on October 2, 2017 that a restaurant in Toronto, Ontario called Kukum Kitchen has started serving a seal meat dish. Although this is an indigenous restaurant, the seal meat comes from a commercial company called SeaDNA therefore has nothing to do with the indigenous hunt. The restaurant claims they are the only restaurant in Toronto that sells seal meat and we do not want this to become a new trend for restaurants. The seal slaughters are very violent, cruel, horrific, traumatizing and unnecessary. They are bludgeoned in the forehead with a tool called a hakipik or shot with a high powered rifle, then cut under their flippers to bleed out. There is blood everywhere and they suffer as alot of them do not die immediately.

> It is 2017 and knowledge is power. We know that our Department of Fisheries and Oceans consider seals adults at only 6 weeks of age. We know that 90% of the seals killed are between 3 weeks to 3 months of age. We know that the killing of innocent beings is wrong. We know that due to global warming, the ice where these beautiful creatures live has been melting and the seal pups are drowning so

> killing them is NOT a matter of population control. We know that they have hearts, brains and feelings just like you and I. These are intelligent beings that do not want to die. Please sign and demand that Kukum Kitchen take seal meat off their menu. Let's protect the seals and keep them off our plates.[8]

A bit of investigative reporting revealed that Jennifer Matos, the petition's linguistically inelegant author, could not explain why she felt an Indigenous restaurant was especially deserving of protest. The City of Toronto apparently has more than 16,000 restaurants, most of which serve meat, and yet Matos naturally feels prone to protest the cuisine of a historically oppressed ethnic minority that was almost destroyed through genocide. Why not start with Italian restaurants that serve veal or French restaurants that serve horsemeat? Is the slaughter and eating of veal (i.e., baby cow) somehow less objectionable than the slaughter and eating of baby seal? [9] Unfortunately, Matos is far from alone. Hollywood celebrities like Paul McCartney and Pamela Anderson have also manifested their racism by calling for an end to seal hunting, as have animal rights' organizations, like PETA.[10] One does wonder if the white people involved realize that in this case, their commitment to animal rights makes them colonial and racist. Regardless, the point should now be clear. The only thing that matters in liberal La La Land is that anything that makes a certain kind of white woman *feel* uncomfortable, ought to be illegal.

*Lesbian and Gay Erasure*

This section of the book has proven the most confusing to write, because of the difficulties involved in addressing trans issues. Second-wave feminists, who are now labeled TERFs by their opponents,[11] maintain that mainstream liberal activism currently reinforces male privilege, because it enables trans-women (i.e., biological males) to dictate (once again) what the social expectations for biological females will be, and even gives biological males license to define who is and is not a woman. This critique of trans-ideology is, admittedly, correct, and illustrates how fucked up mainstream liberalism currently is. Instead of deconstructing and opposing the outward expectations for women's appearance and behavior that have oppressed myriads of women (e.g., being slender, head coverings during worship, lipstick, dresses, high heels, the color pink), by endorsing trans-ideology the Left has reinforced the importance of those expectations. Consequently, different kinds of feminists now war with one another.[12]

Although second-wave feminists do not regards trans-women as women, trans-women are women in the eyes of the White Liberal Matriarchy. Thus, insofar as trans-women are allowed to dictate the rules of the game at the expense of other people's rights, their undeserved and oppressive power can be termed "female privilege." Even if one construes such privilege as male, the disagreements between transwomen and cis-women are still pertinent to this chapter. Safe places for one group create emotional distress for another. This is especially true when transwomen identify as lesbians and expect cis-lesbians to affirm their gender-identity by being open (pun intended) to accepting them as sexual partners. Trans-lesbians seek to break through the "cotton ceiling," often with their male genitalia fully functional and intact, and in reaction cis- (i.e., real) lesbians accuse them of rape.[13] (And yes, the penis of a trans-woman does constitute *male* genitalia, even if the transwoman in question feels oppressed by that assertion.)

To play the provocateur, however, I frame the issue in terms of the White Liberal Matriarchy's perverted exercise of power. At the heart of trans-ideology is the working of something very insidious that wreaks of the WLM's activism, at least in part. The chief question is whether it should be permissible for cis-people to create emotionally unsafe places for trans-people by refusing to recognize their gender identity as valid. Is such refusal part of one's right to free speech? In particularly liberal and totalitarian countries, like Canada, the answer is no.[14] Were it not for the election of Donald Trump in 2016, such liberal totalitarianism would now be reigning in the US. The creeping totalitarianism of pronouns is, however, still gaining ground.

More importantly for our purposes here, the WLM feels that it's wrong for (real) lesbians to define themselves solely in terms of their rejection, not merely of men, but of the penis per se. Instead, (cis-)lesbians should be open to being penetrated sexually by biological males who seek to pass as women. Consider this construal of the issue by Avory Faucette, a trans-activist, for instance:

> Radfems [i.e., real lesbians who are also anti-trans], you're not just missing out on great sex. You're confused about what it means to be a lesbian, or a woman. I don't care what your physical preferences are or what gender identity you prefer. I do care that you confuse those two things, and thereby insult trans-women. I care that you don't bother to interrogate the origins of your phallus-based distaste for trans-women, and think about whether it's actually a dislike of the organ that's happening here or whether transphobia and a refusal to view trans-women as women is

involved. I care that you assume describing yourself as a lesbian tells others that you prefer what you call a pussy, as if everyone has the same definition of *lesbian, woman,* or *pussy.*

THAT is privilege. Assuming that you speak the same language, rather than consensually sharing vocabulary. Using *lesbian* as a proxy term that tells a whole group of women that they are not real, and not seeing anything wrong with that. I find your appropriation of the language of oppression disgusting.

Sit down, shut up, and read a book (or a blog). We will be over here, having fabulous queer sex without you.[15]

Here, Avory promotes the rape culture. He feels that it's not fair that certain lesbians would refuse to have sex with him solely because of his genitalia. He arrogantly assumes that the cis-lesbian rejection of the penis (especially his own) cannot be an innate part of lesbian identity; clearly, it must derive from a lesbian's transphobia. Likewise, Avory is trying to put limits on how others craft their identity. Why shouldn't cis-lesbians be allowed to exclude from their sex lives every single human being who has a penis, just because such a person has a penis? And why are Avory's opponents not entitled to their own definition of *lesbian*? If their recalcitrant, linguistic usage hurts the tranny's feelings, fuck him. If we bring some sanity to this issue, we see that it is a question of the right use of language. If a "lesbian" is open to penile penetration from a transwoman, she ought to be honest and label herself bisexual. As such, Avory's activism constitutes just another attempt at *lesbian erasure.*

By being trans-friendly, the WLM is trying to put limitations on people's rights to say no to someone else's offer of sex. The WLM is also waxing tyrannical by threatening the rights of the rest of us to refuse to affirm that someone else's gender identity is valid. We can't have someone the WLM feels sorry for experiencing rejection, after all. In this, rejected transwomen are like Cindy in chapter 2 of this book. The only thing that matters in the eyes of the WLM is how the (supposedly) oppressed person *feels*. Sexual rejection causes the oppressed to feel more oppressed and should therefore be actively discouraged, even if thereby cis-lesbians are pressured to have sex with trannies against their will. Trans-ideology thus results in the rape and oppression of an already oppressed minority.

In time, the activism of the WLM against lesbians who define themselves in terms of their rejection of the penis, will be used against gay men as well. Chadwick Moore, for instance, has already been deplatformed from Grindr for making it explicitly clear that a hookup app for gay men is no place for trannies. [16] Elsewhere online, one already finds pornography labeled "gay" that includes images of transmen with fully functional female genitalia having sex with cis-men who, if they were honest, would label themselves *bi* and not *gay*. Such porn is gross and is more importantly mislabeled.[17] Virtually no one seeking out *gay* pornography is interested in vaginas. Rejection of the vagina per se is what makes a gay man gay, after all.

The WLM will, of course, react violently to that assertion, but that's not surprising, because a critical mass of heterosexual women have always hated gay men just for being gay. By being gay, we're rejecting women *as such*, and that shouldn't be allowed. It's offensive, misogynist, hurtful to women, and biologically reductionist. Plus, it deprives some women of the heterosexual intimacy and biological children they have to have in order to be happy. In my experience, straight women are on average just as homophobic as straight men, and thus just as prone as straight men to pushing gay men back into the closet and into (usually, but not always) unfulfilling straight marriages. One important factor at work here is how male homosexuality disempowers women. There is no pussy-power in Gay Land; a critical mass of women hate gay men, precisely because gay men cannot be manipulated by heterosexual lust and female charms.

The fact of the matter, however, is that for many gay men, sex really is all about the cock in a way that is often disconnected from the other qualities of the person. Famously, certain gay men, like Milo Yiannopoulos, actively celebrate that aspect of gay identity by fetishizing the black penis. Pro or con, for most homosexuals human sexuality is essentially phallocentric. If the gender confused and their White Liberal Matriarchal allies detest that fact, they can wrap it up and shove it in their bras.

*I bid you to shove your activism into your bra*
*(and not into a certain bodily orifice) not only to*
*insist that you keep your errors to yourself, but*
*more importantly because your **boobs** are small.*

## CHAPTER 6 NOTES

[1] Shay Stewart-Bouley, "Weapon of Lass Destruction: The Tears of a White Woman," *Black Girl in Maine Media* (April 17, 2018), https://blackgirlinmaine.com/racial-and-cultural/weapon-of-lass-destruction-the-tears-of-a-white-woman/.

[2] VK's comments to Luvvie Ajayi, "About the Weary Weaponizing of White Women Tears," *Awesomely Luvvie* (April 17, 2018), https://www.awesomelyluvvie.com/2018/04/weaponizing-white-women-tears.html. Note that the word *bipolar* in square brackets appears in the original.

For more on the power of the tears of white women to perpetuate injustice, see Ruby Hama, "How White Women Use Strategic Tears to Silence Women of Colour," *The Guardian* (May 7, 2018), https://www.theguardian.com/commentisfree/2018/may/08/how-white-women-use-strategic-tears-to-avoid-accountability; and Mamta Motwani Accapadi, "When White Women Cry: How White Women's Tears Oppress Women of Color," *Accapadi* 26, no. 2 (Spring 2007): 208–215, available online, https://files.eric.ed.gov/fulltext/EJ899418.pdf.

[3] Socially conscious sportsmen often work toward the common good by donating the venison they do not want or need to feed the homeless in their area. A quick search on Google for "hunters against hunger" turns up organizations dedicated to that noble goal in at least six States (Illinois, Michigan, Montana, North Dakota, Oklahoma, and South Dakota).

[4] Note that the $135 million every two years is the figure from 2010. For more on it, see http://www.deeralliance.com/node/33. For more on contraceptives for Bambi, see http://www.bowsite.com/bowsite/features/armchair_biologist/immunocontraception/pill1.htm; and http://www.deerfriendly.com/deer-population-control/deer-birth-control-contraception.

[5] Sydney Kashiwagi, "$375K for 150 Days of Work: $4.1M Deer Vasectomy Program Shelling out Huge Salaries," *Silive* (December 17, 2018), https://www.silive.com/news/2018/12/375k-for-150-days-of-work-41m-deer-vasectomy-program-shelling-out-huge-salaries.html.

[6] Ryan Stanton, "Ann Arbor Puts $182K toward Plan to Kill, Sterilize More Deer," *MLIVE* (November 9, 2018), https://www.mlive.com/news/ann-arbor/2018/11/ann_arbor_puts_182k_tow ard_pla.html.

[7] Brian McCombie, "Ineffective Deer Sterilization Programs Cost Taxpayers Millions," *NRA Hunters' Leadership Forum* (July 18, 2019), https://www.nrahlf.org/articles/2019/7/18/ineffective-deer-sterilization-programs-cost-taxpayers-millions/.

[8] [Jennifer Matos,] https://www.thepetitionsite.com/704/964/589/demand-that-kukum-kitchen-in-toronto-ontario-take-seal-meat-off-their-menu/.

[9] Samira Mohyeddin, "Seal Meat Controversy a Reminder That Food Is Used Against Indigenous People," *Vice* (October 16, 2017), https://www.vice.com/en/article/gy547m/seal-meat-controversy-a-reminder-that-food-is-used-against-indigenous-people. See also "Canada Indigenous Restaurant Sparks Debate with Seal Tartare," *BBC News* (October 11, 2017), https://www.bbc.com/news/world-us-canada-41586342.

[10] Julia Whalen, "Seal Meat on the Menu at Toronto Restaurant Sparks Duelling Petitions, Online Debate," *CBC News* (October 11, 2017), https://www.cbc.ca/news/canada/toronto/seal-meat-debate-kukum-1.4347858. Selena Randhawa, "Animal Rights Activists and Inuit Clash over Canada's Indigenous Food Traditions," *The Guardian* (November 1, 2017), https://www.theguardian.com/inequality/2017/nov/01/animal-rights-activists-inuit-clash-canada-indigenous-food-traditions.

[11] Because the term *TERF* was first used as a slur, it is rightly regarded as offensive by second-wave feminists. The term, nonetheless, is becoming more common and some feminists now use it as a means of self-identification. Others prefer the term *vagina feminist* instead. For a glimpse into the violent world of trans-ideology and how the term *TERF* has been used to incite (male) violence against women, see Meghan Murphy, "'TERF' Isn't Just a Slur, It's Hate Speech," *Feminist Current* (September 21, 2017), https://www.feministcurrent.com/2017/09/21/terf-isnt-slur-hate-speech/; Katherine M. Acosta, "Vancouver Panel on Gender Identity and Media Bias Encapsulates Conflict between Women and Trans Activists," *Feminist Current* (November 6, 2019), https://www.feministcurrent. com/2019/11/06/vancouver-panel-on-gender-identity-and-media-bias-encapsulates-conflict-between-women-and-trans-activists/; and Anonymous Guest Contributor, "Dystopian Toronto: Trans Activist Mob Fights to Crush Women's Voices," *Women Are Human* (December 7, 2019), https://www.womenarehuman.com/dystopian-toronto-trans-activist-mob-fights-to-crush-womens-voices/.

[12] Second-wave feminists (of the *Feminist Current* variety) are fascinating, because of the controversies they continue to elicit from the Left. I am grateful to them for their opposition to pornography (especially rape porn) and prostitution, which create an inhumane culture for us all. Most of this book is not addressed to them.

[13] For interesting reactions from second-wave feminists against trans-activism and trans-on-cis rape, see FCM, "The Cotton Ceiling? Really?" *Femonade* (March 13, 2012), https://factcheckme. wordpress.com/2012/03/13/the-cotton-ceiling-really/; Angela C. Wild, *Lesbians at Ground Zero: How Transgenderism is Conquering the Lesbian Body* (March 2019), available online at http://www.gettheloutuk .com/blog/category/research/lesbians-at-ground-zero.html; and Meghan

Murphy, "INTERVIEW: Angela C. Wild of #GetTheLOut on Pride in London and Lesbian Erasure," *Feminist Current* (July 17, 2018), https://www.feministcurrent.com/2018/07/17/interview-angela-c-wild-getthelout-pride-london-lesbian-erasure/.

For a defense of trans-friendly activism on this issue, see "Zoe Degenerate," "The Cotton Ceiling, Reframed," *DeGenerate Diaries* (December 2, 2019), https://degeneratediaries.home.blog/2019/12/02/the-cotton-ceiling-reframed/; and Avory Faucette, "The Cotton Ceiling is Real and it's Time for All Queer and Trans People to Fight Back," *Queer Feminism* (March 27, 2012), https://queerfeminism.com/2012/03/27/the-cotton-ceiling-is-real-and-its-time-for-all-queer-and-trans-people-to-fight-back/.

[14] For an explanation of why people should be free not to recognize someone else's identity as valid, see Meghan Murphy, "What If Your Identity Doesn't Matter at All?" *Feminist Current* (March 22, 2020), https://www.feministcurrent.com/2020/03/22/what-if-your-identity-doesnt-matter-at-all/.

[15] Faucette, "The Cotton Ceiling is Real," https://queerfeminism.com/2012/03/27/the-cotton-ceiling-is-real-and-its-time-for-all-queer-and-trans-people-to-fight-back/.

[16] Chadwick Moore, "Grindr Proves I Was Right about How Charmingly Stupid They Are," *Milo* (July 30, 2018), https://milo.net/45741/grindr-proves-i-was-right-about-how-charmingly-stupid-they-are/; and Chadwick Moore, "Grindr Too Busy to Clear out Aids, Meth and Hookers While There Are Still Republicans to Be Purged," *Milo* (August 2, 2018), https://milo.net/45814/grindr-too-busy-to-clear-out-aids-meth-and-hookers-while-there-are-still-republicans-to-be-purged/.

[17] Here, I do not deny that all pornography is gross.

# Chapter 7
*Insufficiently Infamous Female Frauds*

As should now be clear, the White Liberal Matriarchy typically self-manifests by refusing to submit to objective standards of professionalism, and by demanding that its opponents be censored and silenced. Scrutiny of its visceral calls for "justice" and "equality," however, reveals its incoherence, deceit, obfuscation, and professional fraud. Anna Stubblefield is an important instance of such fraud; her case has already been noted at length. This chapter treats of three other beloved members of the WLM who will probably never be brought to justice and fully revealed as the frauds they are. We begin with Gina Haspel.

## Gina Haspel

Haspel stands at the forefront of our nation's failure to abide by the most basic human rights of all. In Article 1, Section 9 of the US Constitution, our government affirmed the binding nature of habeas corpus, a major concession demanded and won from secular governments by Holy Church in the English Magna Carta of AD 1215. Habeas corpus is a quintessentially medieval (and hence, reasonable) limitation on secular power that requires government officials to put *in writing* the reasons why they think someone's imprisonment or execution is required by the common good.

With the passage of the Eighth Amendment in 1791, our government confirmed another, crucial provision of Magna Carta: the universal prohibition of torture. Because torture cannot be trusted to produce reliable testimony or evidence, it is rightly deemed useless for judicial processes. Most importantly of all, habeas corpus is intended to compel government officials to create a paper trail so that they can be held accountable for the misuse of their power to imprison or kill. As regards the American legal system, consequent to their oath to uphold the Constitution, all elected officials are morally and politically obligated to abide by habeas corpus and the prohibition against torture, even if they do not want to. And note, our government reaffirmed its commitment to the universal prohibition of torture with the ratification of the United Nations' Universal Declaration of Human Rights in 1948, the ratification of the Geneva Convention in 1949, and the ratification of the International Covenant on Civil and Political Rights in 1992.

American political history, however, is blighted by multiple instances in which those in power, including some of our so-called "greatest" presidents, refused to abide by such simple and reasonable limitations on their power. When he signed the Sedition Act of 1798 into law, John Adams, for instance, asserted the right to jail journalists without due process for doing their duty to criticize him and his cronies openly. Abraham Lincoln also systematically imprisoned American citizens without due process during the Civil War for opposing the Union. President Franklin Roosevelt likewise illegally interred Japanese Americans in concentration camps during the Second World War for no reason other than their race and national origin. Finally, George W. Bush was the first president to approve the use of torture and the killing of American citizens without trial to wage the so-called War on Terror. Every president since then has unfortunately imitated

Bush's tyranny. The situation is particularly dire, because all four centuries of American government now offer those in power important, historic precedents to justify the systematic violation of (arguably) the most basic human rights of all.

The guiltiest person at the CIA to oversee and implement the torture thought to be required by the War on Terror is Gina Haspel. The evidence testifying to her guilt is both ample and beyond doubt. And because of President Trump, she served as the Director of the CIA from 2018–2021. [1] Nevertheless, President Obama is also partly responsible for her advancement, for he promoted her to be Director of the National Clandestine Service in February 2013.[2] Her delight in torturing her (our?) enemies goes back to at least 2002. As one commentator has described her criminal misconduct:

> The most well-publicized detainee death happened at the notorious "Salt Pit," a CIA black site, or secret prison, in Afghanistan, where Gul Rahman died of hypothermia after being stripped naked and chained to a wall in near-freezing temperatures. Abuse of prisoners, who were often kidnapped from third [world] countries in a practice known as extraordinary rendition, was rampant at black sites around the world, including Detention Center Green in Thailand, which Gina Haspel ran in late 2002.

> Black site prisoners were hung by chains from ceilings for days on end, stuffed into boxes, deprived of sleep, shackled naked in cold temperatures and subjected to mock executions. Prior to Haspel's arrival, CIA torturers at Detention Center Green

waterboarded the wrong man, a cooperative man, 83 times in a month. In addition to supervising Detention Center Green, Haspel also played a key role in the destruction of videotaped CIA torture sessions.[3]

To get an adequate sense of how unnecessarily inhumane our government's criminal acts are, consider what Khaled el-Masri, an innocent German citizen, endured because he was wrongly thought to be associated with al-Qaeda:

> Believing he was an al-Qaeda militant, Macedonian authorities secretly imprisoned and tortured el-Masri for 23 days before he was blindfolded, handcuffed and handed over to Central Intelligence Agency operatives. He was then stripped, beaten, sodomized, drugged and flown to Afghanistan, where he was imprisoned in the notorious CIA "black site" known as the Salt Pit, where suspected militant Gul Rahman was tortured to death in November 2002.

> El-Masri was held at the Salt Pit and interrogated for four months. During that time, he was never permitted any contact with his family or German government officials. He was never charged with any crime or even brought before a judge.

> Underfed, forced to drink putrid water, denied due process and uncertain if he would ever be released and see his family again, el-Masri went on a hunger strike in March 2004 and lost

60 pounds (27 kg). By the following month, CIA Director George Tenet was informed he was being wrongfully detained. In May, National Security Adviser Condoleezza Rice ordered el-Masri's release.

CIA agents flew el-Masri out of Afghanistan, dumping him on an Albanian roadside without any information or funds to return home to Germany, more than 1,000 miles (1,600 km) away. He was detained by Albanian authorities, who thought he was a terrorist due to his disheveled appearance. When he finally returned home to Ulm, Germany, el-Masri discovered his wife had left for Lebanon with their children because she believed he had abandoned them.[4]

Such acts against an innocent civilian and foreign national justify war. They are also equivalent to rape. Consequently, Haspel's wickedness exceeds that of the man who raped her, or of the man who raped the rape-survivor closest to her. And only the death penalty satisfies the demands of justice in her case. Let the bitch die.

Haspel is a fraud and worse than a rapist. She is clearly unqualified for her position. So why does she have it? WHITE FEMALE PRIVILEGE and fear of making a woman cry has everything to do with it. Close analysis of the propaganda of two of Haspel's defenders clearly backs up that assertion:

To assuage concerns about Ms. Haspel's career, the CIA has offered to make the relevant materials available to the Senate for review behind closed doors. It should resist the request of some senators to declassify her entire personnel file. Since Ms. Haspel spent almost her whole career in clandestine service, was posted overseas on numerous occasions, and ran covert assets against hard targets, such disclosure would be certain to expose sensitive operations, jeopardize the safety of U.S. and allied intelligence agents, and damage national security.

Ms. Haspel has been criticized for her role in the CIA's 2005 destruction of videotapes showing interrogations. At the time, she served as chief of staff to Jose Rodriguez, director of clandestine programs, who authorized the destruction. Given the existence of written transcripts, which included descriptions of the specific interrogation techniques being used, retention of the tapes was not required by law or regulation. There was also justifiable concern that the tapes might be leaked someday, revealing the identity of covert CIA operatives. When Mr. Obama's deputy CIA director, Mike Morrell, investigated the matter, he wrote that he "found no fault with the performance of Ms. Haspel," who had acted "appropriately." Mr. Rodriguez was reprimanded only for not obtaining explicit approval of his superiors before destroying the tapes.[5]

In other words, Haspel ought to be confirmed, because otherwise the career of a women those in power feel sorry for would be ruined. Moreover, bringing the depths of her professional perversion to the public view would make unambiguously clear our government's human rights violations that Haspel herself is partially responsible for. We can't have that, because doing so would make someone's mommy cry.[6]

Curiously, the sordid affair has a silver lining. Senator Dianne Feinstein voted against Haspel, and the Senator's opposition was widely reported in the mainstream media.[7]

Feinstein's statement explaining her vote is worth reading in full. Here are the best parts:

> Ms. Haspel played a central role in the CIA's Rendition, Detention and Interrogation program. This was one of the darkest chapters in our nation's history and it must not be repeated.

> Since her nomination, I and my staff have reviewed thousands of classified documents detailing her role in the program. The takeaway is this: Ms. Haspel was a strong supporter of the torture program.

> While many CIA operatives expressed hesitation or outright opposition to the program, such as John Brennan, Ms. Haspel was not one of them.

> As I said last week, this nomination is bigger than one person. This nomination is about reckoning with our history. It's about grappling with our country's mistakes and making clear to the world that we accept

responsibility for our mistakes and they will never be repeated.

I was struck by Ms. Haspel's repeated insistence at her hearing that the torture program was "legal." The torture program was illegal at the time based on international treaties the United States is signatory to, including the Convention Against Torture and Geneva Convention.

While the Office of Legal Counsel signed off on waterboarding and other "enhanced interrogation techniques," its flimsy legal analyses were withdrawn in 2003 and 2004 and should never have taken precedence over international law.

The bottom line is this: No one has ever been held accountable for the torture program and I do not believe those who were intimately involved in it deserve to lead the agency.

What message does it send to the world if we reward people for presiding over what is considered to be one of the darkest chapters in our history?

...Specifically, her confirmation could complicate U.S.-German relations. While the German government has not made a public position on Ms. Haspel's nomination, Germany is strongly opposed to torture and multiple U.S. intelligence actions outlined in the Senate

Intelligence Torture Report have already caused rifts in U.S.-German relations.

Additionally, when Ms. Haspel was promoted to CIA Deputy Director in 2017, the European Center for Constitutional and Human Rights, headquartered in Berlin, petitioned German prosecutors to order an arrest warrant for Haspel due to her participation in the CIA torture program.

While I understand the German government is unlikely to issue an arrest warrant, Germans still remember that U.S. intelligence officials mistakenly abducted and tortured Khalid al-Masri, a German citizen in 2003.

Mr. Masri, a German citizen, was seized on Dec. 31, 2003, as he entered Macedonia because he was wrongfully believe to be an Al Qaeda terrorist traveling on [a] false German passport.

He was then turned over to the CIA, which rendered, detained and interrogated him. After five months, he was dropped on a roadside in Albania.

This was a grave mistake that even Ms. Haspel acknowledged in a pre-hearing question whether the CIA ever rendered or detained suspects who were innocent by stating: "I understand that the CIA's Office of the Inspector General conducted a review of the

> rendition of Khalid al-Masri and determined that CIA did not meet the standard for rendition under the September 17th, 2001 Memorandum of Notification (MON)."

> Even though the CIA acknowledges this mistake, it is incomprehensible that no one has been held accountable for this and other violations.[8]

I do not particularly like the senior Senator from California, who is surely a devout member of the White Liberal Matriarchy, but by refusing to consent to Haspel's nomination, Feinstein did her duty to defend the Constitution of the United States. She also did her part to divide the WLM against itself. "Divided they fall," as they say.

Unfortunately but predictably, after her nomination Haspel abused her privilege at the CIA by hiring other white, privileged, undeserving, female rapists, just like her.[9] Her foul conduct testifies to the fact that given equal or more-than-equal opportunities, women are just as prone to violence, rape, and cronyism as their male oppressors.

*Fuck patriarchy? Ok. But fuck matriarchy first.*

*Judith M. Bennett*

We turn now to two academics. Judith M. Bennett is noted for studying late-medieval, working-class and/or poor women. Despite the facade of sophistication, she is both a professional fraud and a rape apologist. Here, I analyze her pseudo-intellectual stupidities published in a journal article from the year 2000 regarding the supposed advantages for history writing offered by the label "lesbian-like." [10] The article garnered widespread scholarly attention and was republished in an anthology.[11] It is also based on the plenary address she gave at a conference at CUNY in 1998.[12] An enumeration of Bennett's chief errors follows below:

(1) She claims "lesbian" and "lesbian-like" *cannot* be defined: (a) "No one today is really sure what 'lesbian' means."[13] "Is there such a stable entity as a modern lesbian? Clearly not."[14] (b) "'Lesbian-like' is not a perfect term:...it is as impossible as 'lesbian' to define precisely;...and if over-used, it might even create a lesbian history that lacks lesbians (however defined)."[15] Bennett's failure (or rather, refusal) to define her terms is curious. Every lesbian I've ever talked to knows what a lesbian is. If "lesbian" is per se unclear, perhaps Bennett should explain what she means by the term when she identifies as a lesbian herself. Second, if Bennett's use of the term "lesbian-like" risks generating a history of exclusively heterosexual women, then its use in writing lesbian history is clearly bullshit.

(2) Bennett could have limited her subject matter to lesbians in a more recognizable sense by describing and analyzing known instances of homogenital acts between medieval women, but even an exhaustive treatment of medieval lesbianism in the usual sense of the word would be too short to give modern-day lesbians the medieval history they supposedly want and need. ("If we treat lesbianism as rooted primarily or even exclusively in sexuality, we create very limited histories."[16]) Her failure to delimit her subject matter is unfortunate, because limiting her work to medieval women known to have had sex with other women might have produced a fascinating book or article that needs to be written. But no. That would require actual talent, skill, patience, diligence, and thoughtfulness, attributes she clearly lacks.

(3) Here are the characteristics that get a medieval woman labeled "lesbian-like" by Bennett:

[A] If women had genital sex with other women, regardless of their marital or religious status, let us consider that their behavior was lesbian-like. [B] If women's primary emotions were directed toward other women, regardless of their own sexual practices, perhaps their affection was lesbian-like. [C] If women lived in single-sex communities, their life circumstances might be usefully conceptualized as lesbian-like. [D] If women resisted marriage or, indeed, just did not marry, whatever their reason, their singleness can be seen as lesbian-like. [E] If women dressed as men, whether in response to saintly voices [e.g., Joan of Arc], in order to study, in pursuit of certain careers, or just to travel with male lovers, their cross-dressing was arguably lesbian-like. [F] And if women worked as prostitutes or otherwise flouted norms of sexual propriety, we might see their deviance as lesbian-like.[17]

Of these, only (A) is coherent. The rest refer predominately or exclusively to heterosexual women. As regards (E), if a woman disguised herself as a man so as to accompany her soldier-husband during war, why should she be regarded her as "lesbian-like" at all? Especially if her primary motive for cross-dressing was to continue enjoying mutually-satisfying, straight sex with her husband? As regards (F), a brief conversation with any experienced heterosexual prostitute (e.g., one who has had more than 1,000 male clients) would speedily disabuse Bennett of the error that heterosexual prostitutes have anything in common with lesbians at all.

> *Don't deny it. Deep down on the inside, you know that it was hot for medieval women to dress and pass as men so as to enjoy consensual, mutually satisfying, procreative, vaginal, non-menstrual, straight sex in the missionary position with their husbands outside Lent during wartime; that is, especially if they did so to continue enjoying sex that was positively* **Christian** *and* **normal.**

> *And yes, with the exception of "during wartime," the sex just described is the only kind of sex that* **is** *and* **should be** *normal.*

(4) The one undoubted instance of lesbianism Bennett includes describes the *rape* of one woman by another. She refuses both to call the rapist a lesbian, and to acknowledge the rape as such:

> Laurence, the sixteen-year-old wife of Colin Poitevin, sought a royal pardon from her prison cell. She told a story of how, some two years earlier in her small town of Bleury (near Chartres), she had been seduced by Jehanne, wife of Perrin Goula. The two had walked out to the fields together one August morning, and Jehanne had promised to Laurence that "if you will be my sweetheart, I will do you much good." As Laurence tells it, she suspected nothing evil, acquiesced, and suddenly found herself thrown onto a haystack and mounted

"as a man does a woman." Orgasm followed, certainly for Jehanne, but perhaps also for Laurence who enjoyed herself enough to desire later encounters. In subsequent days and weeks, Laurence and Jehanne had sex together...[multiple times]. But eventually, the affair ended—and violently so, when Laurence's efforts to terminate the relationship caused Jehanne to attack her...Jehanne's fate is unknown; Laurence ended up in prison, whence came the document that today tells her version of their encounters. To us, the behavior of both women is readily labeled lesbian-like...Yet even such clear-cut cases of same-sex relations are not transparent. Laurence cast her plea for clemency in terms as familiar as they were successful; she was a good woman, regretful of her sin, and a victim of an unnatural aggressor [i.e., of a female rapist]. Laurence, who was allowed to return home, reputation secured, after six months in prison, had indulged in a behavior with affinities to modern lesbianisms [i.e., female-on-female rape], but it would be crude to identify her as a 'lesbian' or even as a lesbian-like *person*.[18]

One really must ask how Bennett knows that Laurence desired these sexual encounters at all. Regardless, if Bennett's narrative is an accurate reflection of what happened, it is astounding that she does not label the first sexual encounter *rape*. Laurence, who was only sixteen, "suspected nothing evil, acquiesced, and suddenly found herself thrown onto a haystack and mounted 'as a man does a woman.'" We have here an unambiguous description of non-consensual sex.

Bennett, I imagine, was reluctant to label it *rape*, lest she lend credence to the negative stereotype that lesbians are prone to violence in domestic partnerships. Regardless, by failing to label at least the first sexual encounter "rape," and by implying that it could not have been objectionable if Lawrence wanted more afterwards, Bennett is a rape apologist.

In conclusion, Bennett's "history" is out of touch with reality, because she is out of touch (pun intended) with most (i.e., straight) women. Her label "lesbian-like" is really just her wishful thinking magically transforming historical subjects into potential, imaginary lovers. Crucially, Bennett herself acknowledges that the majority of medieval women she would label "lesbian-like" were heterosexual, and would reject the label if they knew what it meant. As she notes towards the end of her article, "Certainly, many of these women would not have recognized themselves as 'lesbian-like' in any way."[19] Consequently, Bennett's "history" is really just a facile and fatuous exercise in heterosexual erasure. The only identifiable lesbian referred to in her article is a rapist. For that, real lesbians ought to be accusing her of perpetuating homophobia and negative stereotypes regarding queer women.

Despite such bullshit, Bennett has had a very successful academic career and has taught at both the University of Southern California and the University of North Carolina at Chapel Hill. In 1989, she even won a Guggenheim. One off-handed remark, however, reveals the depths of her fraud. After narrating the rape of Laurence quoted above, Bennett says in a footnote,

> The excerpted text can be found in Charles du Fresne du Cange, *Glossarium mediae et infimae Latinitatis* (Paris: Didot, 1844), vol. 3, pp. 663–

664, s.v. "hermaphroditus." I am grateful to Phillipe Rosenberg for his help in reading this text. I have not consulted the full letter (found in Archives Nationales de France, JJ 160:112), but have relied on Edith Benkov's summary of its content.[20]

For those of us with proper training in medieval Latin, such obiter dicta constitute an admission on the part of the author that she can neither read the Latin of the era she purports to study nor has considered in full the historical sources crucial to her so-called "argument." This is fraud through and through, especially when one realizes that by 1981 Bennett had completed an MA and PhD in medieval studies at the University of Toronto, which then as now claims to set the gold standard for academic competence in post-classical Latin, at least in North America.[21] For such rank ignorance and failure to learn the skills basic to her discipline, she ought to be fired.

*Marcie Bianco*

Our final fraud is Marcie Bianco, a journalist and blogger whose work "both online and in print [has appeared] in NBC Think, *Pacific Standard, Quartz, Rolling Stone, Salon, Vanity Fair,* and *Vox,* among other outlets."[22] Her feminism is surprisingly essentialist. A bisexual man who was overwhelmed with incomprehension in response to one of her pieces, has put his finger on the simulacrum of male reality that Bianco apparently thinks characterizes all (heterosexual?) men:

As a snapshot of 2019 America, these stories present a startling picture: Men continue to coerce, harass, rape and kill girls and women—and go to extreme lengths to avoid responsibility for their actions.

...

Men need heterosexuality to maintain their societal dominance over women.

...

Where men seem to never to have to take responsibility for their actions, women always must take responsibility for not only their own actions but the actions of men.

...

While men stew in their mess, women are rising. They are taking back control of their lives and their bodies and they are questioning the foundation of the patriarchy—heterosexuality—that has kept them blindly subordinate for centuries.[23]

The same commentator pinpointed the following parody of womanhood in the same piece:

Women, on the other hand, are increasingly realizing not only that they don't need heterosexuality, but that it also is often the bedrock of their global oppression.

...

Heterosexuality offers women all these things as selling points to their consensual subjection.

...

Historically, women have been conditioned to believe that heterosexuality is natural or innate, just as they have been conditioned to believe that their main purpose is to make babies—and if they fail to do so, they are condemned as not "real," or as bad, women.

...

[Women] are taking back control of their lives and their bodies and they are questioning the foundation of the patriarchy—heterosexuality— that has kept them blindly subordinate for centuries.[24]

One does wonder *which* women and *which* men Bianco has in mind here. The experience of countless sexual minorities proves to the contrary that most gay people cannot just wave a magic wand and change their sexual orientation at will. If they could, conversion therapy might work, but it doesn't. In her own case, apparently, Bianco is a lesbian by choice:

Framed within recent feminist debate, this view is akin to what many call (some do so derisively) "choice feminism." But my understanding of "choice" is not about abundance, but discrimination. To make a choice—to have sex with someone or to identify with a specific sexual orientation— entails judgment. By saying that my sexuality is a choice, I hold myself accountable for all my actions. And to make oneself accountable to both one's self and to others in the world is, I think, the optimal form of a civic-minded ethos.[25]

There's a problem here. Bianco's mind, no doubt, has been deformed by the errors of both Michel Foucault and Judith Butler. And yet, as Martha Nussbaum has shown, Foucault's and Butler's thought is deficient, because it presupposes that human subjects are so imprisoned by the cultural conditioning that forms the substratum of the self that they can never really and fully transcend that conditioning.[26] If, as Bianco claims, heteronormativity is presupposed by the cultural conditioning of us all, including her, how can she so flippantly disregard that conditioning to transmogrify into a lesbian at a moment's notice? Reality is, of course, glaring at her defiantly. Bianco isn't a lesbian at all; she's a bisexual who is repulsed by her attraction to men, and who chooses instead to have sex with only women. In all probability, her lesbian identity, unsteady and Protean as the ocean surf, will perdure only until her womb craves children. Thereafter, she too will go the way of most feminine flesh, and succumb to the dominion of the cock, without which she will die an unloved, childless, old hag in accordance with her demerits. If Bianco refuses to repent of the sin of misandry, that inescapable death by unloved childlessness is positively required by justice. Let the bisexual die unloved.

Nevertheless, if one's sexual orientation is determined by choice and the highest good is maximal freedom to self-actualize provided one respects the rights of others, the question then arises as to Bianco's attitudes towards women who choose to be heterosexual. Their choice to embody heteronormativity and the traditional family through consensual and mutually satisfying straight sex with their husbands and to love one man more than all the rest is not one Bianco can tolerate or accept. Presupposed by her arguments is an essentialism so strict that it requires all women to reject traditional family life, even if that life makes them happy.

*And yes, some women do choose traditional families,*
*because they **want to**, not because they have to.*
*If tying on that apron and making cookies with the kiddos*
*makes some women happy,*
*who are **you** to*
***judge?***

Consequently, Bianco is militantly committed to a suffocatingly restrictive vision of womanhood for all and sundry. For her, *queer* is the only acceptable way for a woman to be. She has chastised white women in the press, for instance, for voting for Donald Trump in 2016, and predictably refuses to tolerate women who dissent from the prevailing trans-ideology.[27] Karen Pence, wife of the Vice President, came under particular fire from Bianco for committing the mortal sin of teaching in a Christian school:

> Mother is heading back to school—haven't you heard?
>
> And it's the latest in the fight for America's soul.
>
> Karen Pence, currently the second lady of the United States, is returning to Immanuel Christian School, a private K-8 elementary school that is a part of the Immanuel Bible Church, to teach art part-time to students.
>
> Civil rights and LGBTQ activists, including most recently Lady Gaga, criticized the SLOTUS's new position because the school explicitly "refuse[s] admission" to students who do not live according to the "biblical

lifestyle"—which means no rough-and-tumble homosexual or bisexual activity. Likewise, the school discriminates against job applicants who do not "live a life of moral purity"; disqualifying conduct includes everything from "lesbian sexual activity" to "transgender identity" to "heterosexual activity outside of marriage."

...

Despite having a lifestyle at least partially funded by the American taxpayer, Karen Pence has the freedom to believe in her evangelical Christian faith; she has the freedom to work at a school that espouses this faith — a faith constructed by a morality that is fundamentally patriarchal, sexist and homophobic. And her freedom to do so is indeed protected by the First Amendment.

...Through a manipulation of First Amendment language, freedom of religion currently serves as code for bigots to justify not only their discriminatory beliefs but the continuation of verbal and physical violence against minority communities. Even though they project the language of the snowflake at civil rights advocates and liberal-leaning citizens, it is they who cry "victim" when their moral values are exposed as promoting hate and violence. Using a quite simple two-pronged logic, they circumvent accountability by projecting blame onto those people who they discriminate against while obfuscating the bigotry of their own beliefs.

...

Here, [feminists Bianco does not accept as feminists] have an unexpected ally in people who perceive Pence's return to the workplace as an equal rights issue. At the Washington Post, opinion writer Alyssa Rosenberg went to far as to herald this return as a "feminist victory" because Pence is "preserving [her] professional independence."

However, a woman entering the workforce is not a feminist victory if the work performed is in the service of bigotry and discrimination. Remember, you cannot divorce the act from the identity. This equation is akin to the mislabeling of white suffragists as feminists. White women who fought for other white women to have the vote, and aligned themselves with racist patriarchs in order to finance their constitutional battle for the 19th Amendment, were not feminists.

Karen Pence is not, contrary to what her defenders say, a victim. Willfully ignorant about the harmful cultural messaging of her actions, and complicit with oppressive systems built on bigoted beliefs, she is the unimpeachable mother—white and heterosexual—who, actually, has always been the idol of "good," Christian, white America. Her defenders are knights in white robes who shout "freedom!" as they cut down their enemy.

This is American history, and, it seems, mother
will continue to teach it.[28]

Bianco's use of the word *mother* is quite revealing. Along with
*Christian, mother* is an identity she will not tolerate in
women. Equally disturbing is Bianco's Marxist-inspired
reading of the US Constitution. Apparently, Mrs. Pence's
"freedom" to practice her religion "is protected by the First
Amendment" but only "through a manipulation of First
Amendment language." How much longer such
"manipulation" is permitted by the courts favorable to
Bianco's political orientation is anyone's guess. In the midst
of so many potential themes for political commentary, one
really must ask why Bianco felt the need to attack Mrs. Pence.
I suspect she did so, because she envies the happiness that
accrues to conservative women, because they are normal.

More surprising, however, than Bianco's intolerance
for normal women, is her opposition to space exploration. As
she described the matter in 2018: Elon Musk and Jeff Bezos

are not only heavily invested in who can get
their rocket into space first, but in colonizing
Mars. The desire to colonize—to have
unquestioned, unchallenged and automatic
access to something, to any type of body, and
to use it at will—is a patriarchal one. Indeed,
there is no ethical consideration among these
billionaires about whether this should be done;
rather, the conversation is *when* it will be done.
Because, in the eyes of these intrepid explorers,
this is the only way to save humanity.

It is the same instinctual and cultural force that
teaches men that everything—and everyone—in

their line of vision is theirs for the taking. You know, just like walking up to a woman and grabbing her by the pussy.

It's there, so just grab it because you can.

...This Columbusing attitude—a strident business acumen laced with an imperialist ethos—comes with an air of benevolence: Musk doesn't just want to colonize Mars to satisfy his ego. No, he wants to colonize Mars to help his fellow humans...In this way, colonizing Mars is a "collective life insurance policy." Although considering the last 500 years of colonization on this planet alone, one could wonder whose lives, according to Musk and other rich white men like himself, are worth being insured...

...The impulse to colonize — to colonize lands, to colonize peoples, and, now that we may soon be technologically capable of doing so, colonizing space — has its origins in gendered power structures. Entitlement to power, control, domination and ownership. The presumed right to use and abuse something and then walk away to conquer and colonize something new.

...This 21st century form of imperialism is the direct result of men giving up on the planet they have all but destroyed.

> As if history hasn't proven that men go from one land to the next, drunk on megalomania and the privilege of indifference.

> The raping and pillaging of the Earth, and the environmental chaos that doing so has unleashed, are integral to the process of colonization. And the connection of the treatment of Mother Earth to women is more than symbolic: Study after study has shown that climate change globally affects women more than men.[29]

Those who wish to read the rest of Bianco's incoherent bullshit are encouraged to do so online. The only point of reading the piece in full is to become apprised of the extent of her hysteria. It takes a distinctive kind of microcephalous idiot to draw a comparison between the European colonization of two continents teeming with millions of people and human migration to a planet that, as far as we know, supports no sentient life forms.[30] Apparently, men are evil, because only they are responsible for the destruction of the environment. As one blogger has noted, Bianco's analogy likewise fails, because white, European, male exploitation of the Americas did not occur after men had destroyed the European environment.[31] Nevertheless, while summarizing one of Bianco's "points," the same blogger has salvaged something worth thinking about from her incoherent dribble:

> Enterprise, technological achievement, courage, initiative, the opening of new possibilities for mankind, the extension of the reach of human civilization, the willingness to take risk, the drive to explore, and the passion

to build are all bad things, impertinent, hubristic expressions of intrinsically wicked patriarchy.[32]

Although the nouns listed at the beginning of this quotation are not bad or hubristic, they are attributes of men at their best. Because Bianco so hates men that she wants us all to cease to exist or to choose to become queer women, she also hates all the things that make men godlike, like the urge to expand the realm of human possibilities beyond the stars.

For her hate speech demonizing so much that is laudable and ennobling in women, men, and in human nature generally, Marcie Bianco ought to be fired and publicly shamed for being the soul-sucking, uncultured, degrading, and unprofitable leech she is. I have yet to unearth the depths of her fraud, however. The apocalypse begins now.[33] Consider how she describes herself online:

> Bianco has an undergraduate degree in Government from Harvard (cum laude); a MSt in Women's Studies from the University of Oxford (Hertford College); and a MA and a PhD in English Literature from Rutgers University. Her academic publications in journals and book collections run the gamut, from Christopher Marlowe to Gertrude Stein, trans-inclusive feminism to pop culture poetics. She has taught literature, composition, and social justice courses at a number of higher education institutions, including Rutgers University, Fordham University, John Jay College, and Hunter College.[34]

The extent of her accomplishments is jaw-dropping, especially when one realizes the superficiality of her "thought," as evidenced in this chapter. The stultifying tastelessness of her prose testifies to the fact that she never learned to write or think properly, despite attending schools that claim to be among the world's finest. Her mental constipation and verbal diarrhea, and the bibliography at the end of her doctoral dissertation also lead one to the conclusion that her literary persona is horrid, because she never developed proficiency in even a single foreign language. [35] As noted in my treatment of Stubblefield, ignorance of foreign languages first belies the colonialism, racism, and xenophobia historically presupposed by the American "educational" system; and second, the latent racism, colonialism, xenophobia, and narrowness more generally of the products of that system who refuse to put in the time and effort necessary to correct the defects of the "educational" system that produced them. Demonstrable foreign-language ability, ideally in at least one ancient and one modern language, should be a mandatory prerequisite for any serious, full-time academic position in the humanities, and perhaps in the professorate simply. Only with foreign-language expertise is intercultural exchange actually possible on the terms of the non-English-speaking other. Contrariwise, embodying the expectation that the whole world learn English so as to serve the *white woman* on *her* terms is an unacceptable way of being. Given that Marcie Bianco has had numerous opportunities to learn a foreign language but has not availed herself of them, her willful ignorance embodies that unacceptable and colonial way of being, and ought to disqualify her from being taken seriously qua academic, and qua human. Unfortunately but predictably, precisely because of her self-centered sloth, myopic parochialism, colonialism, and parrot-like, unthinking, dogmatic, feminist chatter, she holds degrees from both Harvard and Oxford.

In sum, because of the WHITE, FEMALE, AND UNDESERVED PRIVILEGE that Marcie Bianco has always benefited from, she pollutes the intellectual air with the fetid stench of her incoherent, feminist, and Marxist dogmatism wherever she might go, like the putrid-smelling, rain-drenched, and feral bitch she is.

## CHAPTER 7 NOTES

[1] For the use of torture to advance American foreign policy in detail, see Spencer Ackerman, "Inside the Fight to Reveal the CIA's Torture Secrets," *The Guardian* (September 9, 2016), https://www.theguardian. com/us-news/2016/sep/09/cia-insider-daniel-jones-senate-torture-investigation.

[2] https://en.wikipedia.org/wiki/Gina_Haspel.

[3] Brett Wilkins, "A Brief History of American Torture," *Counterpunch* (May 8, 2018), https://www.counterpunch.org/2018/05/08/a-brief-history-of-american-torture/.

[4] Brett Wilkins, "Macedonia Apologizes to Innocent German Seized and Tortured by CIA," *Antiwar.com* (April 11, 2018), https://original.antiwar.com/brett_wilkins/2018/04/10/macedonia-apologizes-to-innocent-german-seized-and-tortured-by-cia/.

[5] David B. Rivkin Jr. and Lee A. Casey, "What's at Stake in the Attack on Haspel," *The Wall Street Journal* (May 8, 2018), A15, available online at http://davidbrivkin.com/whats-at-stake-in-the-attack-on-haspel/.

[6] NPR's reporting of the story is of interest. See Bill Chappell, "'I Don't Believe That Torture Works,' CIA Nominee Gina Haspel Tells Senators," *NPR* (May 9, 2018), https://www.npr.org/sections/thetwo-way/2018/05/09/609681289/gina-haspel-confirmation-hearing-cia-nominee-faces-senators-questions; and Greg Myre, "Senate Panel Approves Gina Haspel as CIA Chief; Confirmation Appears Likely," *NPR* (May 16, 2018), https://www.npr.org/sections/parallels/2018/05/16/611574553/senate-panel-approves-gina-haspel-as-cia-chief-confirmation-appears-likely.

[7] Joe Garofoli, "Dianne Feinstein Says She Will Vote against Gina Haspel as CIA Chief," *San Francisco Chronicle* (May 10, 2018), https://www.sfchronicle.com/politics/article/Dianne-Feinstein-says-she-will-vote-against-Gina-12904845.php; Jeremy Herb, "Feinstein Says She's 'Very Wary' of Haspel as CIA Director," *CNN Politics* (March 23, 2018), https://www.cnn.com/2018/03/23/politics/dianne-feinstein-gina-haspel-cia-director/index.html; Emily Tillett, "Feinstein Says Gina Haspel's Role in Torture Program 'Not Necessarily Appropriate' for CIA Top Spot," *CBS News* (April 22, 2018), https://www.cbsnews.com/news/feinstein-says-gina-haspels-role-in-torture-program-not-necessarily-appropraite-for-cia-spot/; and "Senate Votes to Confirm Gina Haspel as 1st Female CIA Director," *Fox News* (May 17, 2018), https://www.fox4news.com/news/senate-votes-to-confirm-gina-haspel-as-1st-female-cia-director.

[8] Dianne Feinstein, "Feinstein Votes 'No' on Gina Haspel Nomination," https://www.feinstein.senate.gov/public/index.cfm/press-releases?ID=F17837BE-A634-4AF6-B40E-3BF5412424FE

[9] "The CIA's first female director since its 1947 founding, [Haspel] has put in place her own leadership team—which also includes many

women—and so far has avoided having President Trump's political allies embedded in the agency's senior ranks." Warren P. Strobel, "Haspel's CIA Steps Out of the Limelight," *The Wall Street Journal* (May 28, 2019), A4. The online version is entitled, "Under CIA Chief Ginal Haspel, an Intelligence Service Returns to the Shadows," and can be found here: https://www.wsj.com/articles/under-cia-chief-gina-haspel-an-intelligence-service-returns-to-the-shadows-11558776600.

[10] Judith M. Bennett, "'Lesbian-Like' and the Social History of Lesbianisms," *Journal of the History of Sexuality* 9, no. ½ (January–April 2000), 1–24.

[11] Judith M. Bennett, "'Lesbian-Like' and the Social History of Lesbianisms," in *The Feminist History Reader*, ed. Sue Morgan, (London: Routledge, 2006): 244–259.

[12] The conference is noted on Bennett's CV, available on her website, https://dornsife.usc.edu/cf/faculty-and-staff/faculty.cfm?pid=1008252.

[13] Bennett, "'Lesbian-Like' and the Social History of Lesbianisms," *Journal of the History of Sexuality* 9, no. ½ (January–April 2000), 10.

[14] Ibid., 13.

[15] Ibid., 21.

[16] Ibid., 16.

[17] Ibid., 15.

[18] Ibid., 18–19.

[19] Ibid., 23.

[20] Ibid., 19, footnote 47.

[21] Her degrees are listed on her CV, already noted. ProQuest Dissertations & Theses Global lists her dissertation thus: Judith Mackenzie Bennett, "Gender, Family and Community: A Comparative Study of the English Peasantry, 1287–1349" (PhD diss., University of Toronto, 1981).

[22] http://marciebianco.com/about/.

[23] Marcie Bianco, "Miley Cyrus' Split with Liam Hemsworth Isn't Just Celebrity Gossip—It's a Blow to the Patriarchy," *Think* (August 16, 2019), https://www.nbcnews.com/think/opinion/miley-cyrus-split-liam-hemsworth-isn-t-just-celebrity-fodder-ncna1042931. These passages are quoted here: u/brother_meowzone, "Marcie Bianco, Feminism, Patriarchy," https://www.reddit.com/r/bisexual/comments/csp911/marcie_bianco_feminism_patriarchy/.

[24] Ibid.

[25] Marcie Bianco, "Yes, My Sexuality is a Choice: Why I Reject the 'Born This Way' Narrative," *Salon* (May 15, 2016), https://www.salon.com/2016/05/14/yes_my_sexuality_is_a_choice_why_i_reject_the_born_this_way_narrative/.

[26] Martha C. Nussbaum, "The Professor of Parody: The Hip Defeatism of Judith Butler," *The New Republic* (February 22, 1999), https://newrepublic.com/article/150687/professor-parody.

[27] Marcie Bianco, "White Women Voted for Trump in 2016 Because They Still Believe White Men Are Their Saviors," *Quartz* (November 14, 2016), https://qz.com/835567/election-2016-white-women-voted-for-donald-trump-in-2016-because-they-still-believe-white-men-are-their-saviors/. Marcie Bianco, "Feminists Are Now Fighting Each Other over What Defines a Real Woman," *Quartz* (June 9, 2015), https://qz.com/423568/feminists-are-now-fighting-each-other-over-what-defines-a-real-woman/.

[28] Marcie Bianco, "Karen Pence, LGBTQ Discrimination and the Christian Right's Embrace of Victimhood," *Think* (January 22, 2019), https://www.nbcnews.com/think/opinion/karen-pence-lgbtq-discrimination-christian-right-s-embrace-victimhood-ncna961066.

[29] Marcie Bianco, "The Patriarchal Race to Colonize Mars Is Just Another Example of Male Entitlement," *Think* (February 21, 2018), https://www.nbcnews.com/think/opinion/patriarchal-race-colonize-mars-just-another-example-male-entitlement-ncna849681.

[30] The expression "microcephalous idiot" I found in E. Belfort Bax, *The Fraud of Feminism* (London: Grant Richards, 1913), 7, available online at https://archive.org/details/fraudoffeminism00baxerich/page/6/mode/2up.

[31] David Zincavage, "Space Travel = Colonialism & Male Entitlement," *Never Yet Melted* (February 22, 2018), https://neveryetmelted.com/2018/02/22/space-travel-colonialism-male-entitlement/.

[32] Ibid.

[33] Here, I use the word *apocalypse* in its original Greek meaning of *unveiling*.

[34] http://marciebianco.com/about/.

[35] Marcie Bianco, "The Spirit of Marlowe: Creating an Ethics on the English Renaissance Stage," (PhD diss., Rutgers University, 2012), 278–294.

# Chapter 8
*What We Can Do*

"The future is female," as a friend recently remarked to me by email. That depressing forecast is correct, if right-thinking men and our female allies do not take matters into our own hands and militantly fight against the WHITE, FEMALE, AND UNDESERVED PRIVILEGE of women like those I have pilloried in this book. This chapter brings the current jeremiad to its end with a list of practical suggestions for toppling and subverting the matriarchy. It concludes with an observation that should make the White, Liberal Matriarchy squirm with discomfort and self-distrust.

A single question lurks behind every page of this book that must now be addressed nudely: *What do women actually want?* I have argued that whereas women *say* they want equality, in fact they want privilege; that is, they actually want the very *opposite* of what they *say* they want. The advice given below encourages conservative activists to be creative about finding ways to *compel* women to accept the equality they have demanded even in those moments when they will not benefit therefrom. To win this war, we must learn afresh the importance of shame and practice the courage to demand equal justice, including equal punitive justice, under the law. In other words, get creative when it comes to enforcing the same standards against women that women demand against men.

*Equal Punishment for Female Rapists*

When the behavior of a woman meets the legal definition of sexual harassment, rape, and/or child abuse, openly shame her for her inability and/or failure to control her cunt, compare her to the man who raped her or caused her the most harm, and in general advocate the death penalty for rapists, including male rapists, or at least for repeat offenders. Contrary to what the contemporary church would have us believe, if someone representing the authority of the state were to put a bullet through the skull of a rapist, and splatter her brains on the sidewalk, the world would become a better place thereby. Do not relent even if those lecherous, sexually-violent bitches start weeping. Point out that their cunts are just as threatening to other people's welfare as Brett Cavanaugh's or Donald Trump's erect dick. Turn the rapist's *vagina* back into the *pudenda*.

> *You do not and should not have the right to*
> *act that way and go unpunished,*
> *you worthless piece of menstruating swine*
> *shit!*

As the Bret Cavanaugh case shows, mainstream feminism has endorsed a kind of public shaming so intense for male rapists that the women in power literally

126

do not care if shaming the male criminal results in his suicide. Given that standard of unrelenting, punitive justice imposed decades after a rape was committed *by a minor*, seek out opportunities to shame female rapists intensely and mercilessly. An essential part of such shaming should be openly expressing the desire that such shame should permanently erode the mental health of the female criminal. If such psychological degradation results in suicidal depression, that's just what she gets not merely for *doing* something wrong, but more importantly, for *being* the worthless piece of shit she just radically *is*. And yes, failure to control a single urge in a single moment of temptation should result in lifelong punishment, because that's the standard women use to judge and shame men for rape.

Our holy, Catholic religion unambiguously teaches that rapists, regardless of sex and/or gender, justly burn in hell forever if they die impenitent. Do not neglect to include threats of literal hellfire in your shaming. Strange to say, those who come to the defense of a female rapist whose guilt is manifest are acting in ways that are chivalrous, and hence essentially patriarchal, which feminists say they do not want. Condemn such behavior as *patriarchal* and threaten such persons with hellfire for standing in the way of the punishment demanded by justice. Compare such hellfire to rape at the hands of the God who thinks that impenitent rapists are not worth saving.[1]

*You say you do not want patriarchy, but in fact you do! The alternative to patriarchy is*

*no knight in shining armor (or anyone else*
*for that matter) coming to save you.*

Insist that rape in women is unforgiveable, precisely because women will not forgive the same sin in men. As the Lord Jesus taught us,

> For if ye forgive men their trespasses, your heavenly Father will also forgive you. But if ye forgive not men their trespasses, neither will your Father forgive your trespasses...Judge not, and ye shall not be judged. For with what judgment ye judge, ye shall be judged: and with what measure ye mete, it shall be measured to you again. (Matt. 6:14–15; 7: 1–2)[2]

Hence, God himself has solemnly promised to forgive us *only as* we forgive others. Insofar as women refuse to forgive male rapists, when women are guilty of rape, they literally *cannot* be forgiven. Because God has solemnly promised not to forgive them, the rest of us are under no obligation to forgive them either.

*That's just what you get...*
*for failing to control your cunt.*
*And it doesn't matter if you did it only once.*
*Your guilt remains forever.*

Insist that the legal definition of rape be uniformly enforced, even if and even when women disagree and/or reject that definition for a good reason. For instance, if a wealthy and powerful woman fraudulently offers a man a job she cannot give him on condition that he have sex with her, she is guilty of rape by deception under California State law if they have sex. If women who are guilty of such "rape," object to being labeled rapists, point out that by labeling them as such, you are merely demanding that a law be enforced that is on the books only because *women want it to be*. Note also that the law is binding, even if women find it oppressive, and even if some who break it are honestly ignorant of what it requires. *Ignorantia legis non excusat*, as the ancient Romans taught us. The whole point of law is, after all, to restrict people's freedom to do bad things.

*Equal Freedom to Say No to Someone Else's Offer of Sex*

As hinted at in chapter 2 of this book, women have claimed the right to refuse a man's offer of sex for any reason or no reason at all. "Any reason" includes reasons that are *racist, classist,* openly degrading, and/or *intentionally* hurtful. It remains for men to claim the same right and to do women, including emotionally vulnerable women, what white women of privilege do to men all the time. Learn the art of practicing virtue by saying no in ways that are *intended* to be hurtful *and* degrading. While saying no, make it clear that you're saying no, *because* she (or he) is fat, white, black, ugly, poor, rich, Asian, Chelsea Clinton, a Packers fan, liberal, too conservative, refuses to celebrate Father's Day, likes country music, voted for Hilary, and/or has small boobs. "Any reason" includes *any* reason, however arbitrary or intentionally hurtful.

While talking about these issues in a merely theoretical way, remind people that white woman of privilege, like Chelsea Clinton, have asserted the right to refuse a black man's offer of sex just because he's black. In light of that racist precedent, which no member of the WLM can reasonably deny, assert the right to say no to a transwoman, *just because the transwoman is trans.* If someone objects that refusing to have sex with a trans person *because* the trans person is trans ought to be illegal, because thereby one is refusing to acknowledge the trans person's gender identity as valid, assert that any limitations on one's *right* to say *No* perpetuates the rape culture.

In other words, the right to say *No* necessarily includes the right to cause *demonstrable harm* while saying *No,* even in those moments when the demonstrable harm results in someone's suicide. This includes the right to reveal that one is saying no, because one thinks the person being rejected is inherently unworthy of love (in the sense of long-term, emotionally-satisfying intimacy). If men are to be forced to learn to respect the rights of women when women reject them, women should be forced to do the same to men. If being turned down shoves a woman into the abyss of suicidal depression, that does not matter. The man who said *No* was merely acting within his rights when he did so. Any limitations whatsoever on a man's right to say *No* are unacceptable because any such limitations *perpetuate the rape culture.*

*You don't have a right to my body,*

*even in those moments when you'll fucking*
*kill yourself if I don't let you*
**suck my dick, bitch.**

The question is one of *rights*, not of ethics. But then again, to approach the issue ethically, one must acknowledge that adultery is always wrong, even if there is no other way to help someone avoid suicide. Thus, men, grow up! If she's not your wife say no, *and let that adulterous bitch die.* And notice: if she has to have adultery to avoid suicide, God himself thinks she's not worth saving.

## Free Speech and Verbal Violence

Especially in the context of free speech on university campuses, assert and apply the adage that "verbal violence is just as bad as physical violence" when women are verbally violent. Such verbal violence is often apparent when the White Liberal Matriarchy tries to censure pro-life speech. To censure their opponents, mainstream feminists typical assert things like "there exists a right to free speech, but there also exists a right not to be intimidated, belittled, and silenced," [3] but intimidation, belittling, and silencing is precisely what the White Liberal Matriarchy does to its opponents in the name of creating and maintaining emotionally safe places for its members. Consequently, when women are verbally violent and thereby try to censure conservative speech, openly compare them to physically violent men. For example, if a liberal woman starts screaming at a prolife protestor, openly compare her to the man who beat her, because she, just like her abuser, cannot control her urges.

An anecdote from my own life testifies to the kind of violence to which liberal women are prone in the face of arguments regarding abortion. While studying Latin in Rome one summer, I tried to engage in reasoned, civil discourse with one of my fellow students. We were eating at a restaurant that was large by Italian standards and crowded. I prefaced my comments by asking, "Are you sure you want to know what I think about this? I'm pretty sure you won't like what I have to say." She answered yes. I then proceeded to give what I take to be the pro-life position. Unexpectedly, my illiberal-liberal opponent let fly her rage and just started screaming. After overcoming my initial incomprehension at her irascibility, I got up and proceeded to leave. When I was almost at the door, she momentarily stopped screaming and asked what I was doing. I replied, "I'm leaving, because I refuse to waste my time being screamed at by a bitch like you." Thereat, she began pounding the table with her fists and banging the bottom of the table with her kneecaps, shouting in a restaurant full of people, "YOU CAN'T EMBARRASS ME LIKE THIS." Well, actually I can. And I would perpetuate that embarrassment here, if I knew her name. Apparently, in liberal La La Land, someone like me has no choice but to remain present while being screamed at by his liberal, female betters.

Let's analyze what happened in that exchange. I went out of my way to obtain a woman's *consent*, and then gave her *exactly* what she consented to. She then responded with verbal violence that triggered unpleasant memories in me of being verbally abused as a boy by someone just as irascible as she is. Because of her verbal violence, my interlocutor is thus comparable to a child abuser; she is also comparable to a woman who clearly and unambiguously consents to sex with a man, but who then accuses him of rape afterwards because she woke up the next day feeling used sexually and dirty. What, after all, is a false accusation of rape other than punishing someone for giving you what you have asked for? Naturally, because of WHITE FEMALE PRIVILEGE, when women make such false accusations, they are almost never held responsible for their misconduct, although they should be punished with jail time. Because the altercation happened in a restaurant, her behavior also resembles that of a woman who starts screaming, because a waiter brought her the food she ordered. The fault, of course, does not lie with the waiter; it lies with the woman who is screaming, because she will not come to terms with the fact that she ordered the wrong thing. Because of WHITE FEMALE PRIVILEGE, however, people wrongly feel pity for the maenad and blame instead the man who gave her what she *said* she wanted. In this case, despite other students from the Latin school being present and witnessing her consent to my request for discourse, no one objected to her verbally abusive behavior. As far as I know, she suffered no negative consequences at all other than the embarrassment of being publicly revealed as the abuser she is.

Thoughtful reflection upon that incident offers curious insights into the nature of sex and academic discourse. Both are inherently risky endeavors. Discourse can be pleasurable and result in the conception and birth of new ideas, and ideally of wisdom, in the soul; it can also result in permanent harm.

**Woe** *to those in whom* **Wisdom** *is* **aborted.**

Likewise, to be ethical, discourse must always be consensual. But consensual discourse need not be pleasurable; it too sometimes causes harm. Nonetheless, if consensual discourse does in the end prove to be harmful, qua consensual, it is still ethical, and the person thereby harmed has no grounds for complaint. She has merely received what she consented to, after all.[4] As regards university life, contrary to what lovers of emotionally-safe places feel, universities are suppose to enable and encourage consensual truth-seeking, even when harm results therefrom. Contrariwise, safe places prevent people from developing the emotional and rational skills needed to engage in civil discourse. So why did my interlocutor scream at me? She did so, in part because she's lived in liberal and emotionally safe places her whole life that have never forced her to develop the skills necessary to treat her opponents fairly.

At issue here is the ability to remain present while fighting fairly when an opponent brings forth rhetorically powerful arguments that threaten truth-claims one deems to be sacred, including truth-claims about one's so-called "rights." So often, people lack that ability, because they've never been forced to develop it. It is absolutely essential, however, to being fully human. Without the ability to remain present while fighting fairly in the midst of conflict, one cannot have a romantic relationship in one's private life that will be successful in the long run. Nor can one be political in any classically recognizable sense of that term. Because academic life *should* enable controversial, political discourse, without the ability to remain present while fighting fairly, one cannot really be an academic either, in the ideal sense of that word.

> *Hate it or love it, a fully human life is*
> *impossible without conflict, disagreement,*
> *and risk-taking. The fact that a certain risky*
> *behavior hurt you, does not change the fact*
> *that **I obtained your consent beforehand**.*

Verbal violence can also be termed "emotional incontinence." It takes on a variety of forms. As noted in chapter 5, women are prone to verbal violence in the doctor's office when doctors do their duty to deliver accurate, but unfortunate diagnoses. If verbally abusive patients refuse to apologize to the doctor for their misconduct, the due penalty for their violence should be to be denied basic medical care even in an emergency. Women are also prone to verbal violence while defending those they "love." For instance, the film *Dogville* (2003) provides an excellent example of a distinctively feminine form of verbal violence directed unjustly at a female rape survivor. After the film graphically depicts the rape of Grace, played by Nicole Kidman, the rapist's wife openly shames Grace for supposedly deserving to be raped. Naturally, the rapist's wife just *feels* that her husband cannot *really* be guilty. Thus, if he did rape Grace, she must somehow have deserved it, probably by being a slut who tempted him. At the end of the film, Grace is vindicated, when both the rapist and his verbally abusive wife are executed together and in the same way for their violence. Thereby, the film sends the message that yes, verbal violence from women is sometimes *just* as bad as rape from men. Because both forms of violence are *equally* despicable, both deserve the same penalty at the hands of the state, in this case, the death penalty. The film thus encourages us to cry foul when women, out of a twisted kind of perversion they mislabel *love*, defend their worthless-piece-of-shit husbands, boyfriends, or fathers by verbally degrading their victims.

> *You are responsible for your acts, Ma'am,*
> *even when you don't want to be,*
> *even in the midst of feelings of perversion*
> *you **mislabel** "love."*

*Equality in University Admissions and Hiring*

Insist that women (and their male allies) who lack the emotional maturity necessary to engage in rape discourse are unfit for university life. Their admission to university, especially to elite universities, is unjust, because it deprives more qualified (mostly male) candidates of what is theirs by right.

Make known the statistics regarding university graduation rates. In the US, more women than men have been graduating from college since 1982. Since 2014, there have been more women with university degrees in the population at large than men with university degrees. Point out how women are often offered prestigious university jobs solely because of their gender. Point out as well that the majority of university professors in the humanities are now women. For instance, of the faculty listed on the website of the Department of Classical Studies at the University of Michigan at Ann Arbor, 61% are women.[5]

When privileged, white women claim that relieving the oppression of (mostly poor) women from the developing world requires privileging other privileged, white women even more, ask them to explain *how exactly* the white women *of their class* are more oppressed than their male peers. Despite what they *feel*, the system is now prejudiced in their favor as regards higher education, job markets, custody battles, incarceration rates, and suicide rates. One really must ask why. If they assert that *all* women *solely in virtue of their gender* are more oppressed than *all* men, ask them to explain *how exactly* Chelsea Clinton *solely in virtue of her gender* is more oppressed than men who are black, gay, homeless, uninsured, HIV-positive, and suicidal.

Ask the White, Liberal Matriarchy to define what it means by equality and what an equal world would actually look like. Tell them the following anecdote:

> When asked how many of the nine judges on the US Supreme Court should be female—and at what point there would be enough women on the bench, Ruth Bader Ginsburg had a simple answer: "When there are nine." An all-female Supreme Court? Why not, in her view.[6]

Then ask them to explain how 9 can equal 0.

*Equality at Work and in Shared Spaces*

When women prove to be grossly incompetent at work, demand that they be fired. To refer to an anecdote in my own life discussed in chapter 5, if someone's granny proves to be so utterly incompetent that despite her best efforts, she cannot learn how to attach a file to an email, make a fuss, and point out both to her and to her supervisor that if she were male, she would have been fired weeks earlier. Keep in mind that we lost the political campaign I volunteered on, precisely because the man in charge refused to fire a woman for that kind of incompetence. The fact is, her inclusion was not worth the price of losing the campaign. If a woman begins to weep when she learns that she's lost her job for rank incompetence, point out that her crying at work also reveals her unfitness for the position.

Insist that people practice basic hygiene in shared spaces. If a woman expects others to clean up her vaginal flow in a bathroom that other people are paying rent to use, she ought to be castigated openly for her lack of basic hygiene. If she refuses to clean up her unhygienic mess in the future, she ought to be kicked out. If being kicked out means homelessness, then so be it. More generally, equality requires holding women responsible for misconduct due in whole or in part to menstruation. Reluctance to cause a woman embarrassment or shame for misconduct while she bleeds is quintessentially patriarchal.

*As an Aside*

One does wonder why men refuse to wake up and treat the WLM *precisely as* it treats men. One reason that prevents the necessary reform is heterosexual desire. Straight men are naturally at a disadvantage in such conflict, because they're typically enslaved to their lusts. Surely, we can all imagine a man's wife or girlfriend retaliating at home with sexual frigidity, because he fought for men's rights (including his own) with the White, Liberal Matriarchy, and thereby hurt the feelings of women his wife or girlfriend feels sorry for. Although being gay does put me at a disadvantage in so many respects, it nevertheless frees me up to wage these battles. Being gay is a form of misogyny, after all. It's about rejecting women, qua women, just because they're women.

*If you bitches don't like it,*
*you can storm off and **fuck yourselves**.*

*What Women Want*

We now come to the most offensive and potentially dangerous suggestion of this book. What women actually want is so often exactly the opposite of what they *say* they want. To illustrate:

*What Woman Say They Want*

- Monogamy
- My opinions

- An accurate diagnosis
- Free speech
- A wide spectrum of viewpoints
- The same standards of professionalism
- A legal definition of rape so comprehensive that it makes some women rapists
- Respect for human rights
- Respect for gays
- Respect for lesbians
- Respect for gays and lesbians
- Multiculturalism and Post-colonialism
- Respect for Native American cultures
- Equal political power
- For men and women to honor each other
- For men to be in touch with their feelings
- Cleanliness

*What Women Actually Want*

- An open relationship if required to help someone avoid suicide
- Me to keep my mouth shut
- To live in the bliss of ignorance regarding their cancer
- Censorship of conservative dissent
- Institutions that are emotionally safe because discourse is censored
- Much lower standards for university admission and employment
- Definition of rape to be used only against men
- Torture overseen by women at the CIA
- Gays to pretend to be straight by being willing to have sex with transmen with vaginas

- Lesbians to pretend to be straight by being willing to have sex with transwomen with penises
- Homosexual erasure on the altar of trans-activism
- Everyone in the world to learn English, so as to serve and please the white woman on *her* terms (i.e., *colonialism*)
- The hunting and meat-eating essential to Native American cultures to be made illegal
- Only women on the Supreme Court
- The abolition of Father's Day
- The end of patriarchy
- No man
- For men to practice "chivalry" and to intervene at a moment's notice to save women who are guilty of grave crimes from being punished in accordance with their demerits (i.e., a benign, beneficial patriarchy)
- For men never to express (the feeling of) anger (at least towards women)
- A man in their private life to give them the heterosexual intimacy and/or biological children necessary for their happiness
- Others to clean up their vaginal flow

In short, throughout the course of this book, we have seen that women *say* they want *equality*, but they actually want *privilege*, exactly the opposite of the equality they *say* they want. Unfortunately, one historic stereotype that men have used to oppress women and to perpetuate the rape culture presupposes that irrational bifurcation when it comes to sex:

> She **says** she does not want to have sex,
> but **in fact** she does.

That stereotype must, of course, be condemned along with the men who use it to justify rape. And yet, given how often what women *say* they want fails to correspond to what they *actually* want, that oppressive stereotype might seem to be sometimes reasonable. For me, this isn't a problem, because gay men can be trusted both to know what they want sexually and to verbalize it. Women, on the other hand, are a mass of confusion. *Why are white women so reluctant to be honest about what they actually want?* Answer: They're reluctant to hurt someone's feelings and thereby to appear rude in the sight of other people. And sometimes they don't even know what they want. That is all. Because such reluctance amounts to outright lying and perpetuates the rape culture, it is not ethically permissible.

*Hurtful rudeness is necessarily preferable to dishonesty.*

The White Liberal Matriarchy, however, refuses to acknowledge that fact for what it is. Doing so would threaten its power.

**CHAPTER 8 NOTES**

[1] I do, of course, believe that there are rapists in heaven who repented.

[2] I quote from the King James (Authorized) Version of 1611 to play with the ambiguities inherent in the English word *man*. I realize that here *man* refers to "human being in general" and not to "male human being," but the double entendre is required by context.

[3] Megan Fitzgerald, "Bettina Arndt Should Not Be on Campus: Free Speech Is Not an Absolute Right," *Honi Soit* (September 10, 2018), https://honisoit.com/2018/09/op-ed-bettina-arndt-should-not-be-on-campus/.

[4] Because historically *person* is a feminine noun, the pronouns that refer to it ought to be feminine, as in this sentence.

[5]https://lsa.umich.edu/classics/people/departmental-faculty.html#q=&alpha=&page=1&tag=&tagns=&tagtext=&time=1605190897188

[6] Carla Bleiker, "US Supreme Court Justice Ruth Bader Ginsburg, a Champion of Women's Rights," *DW* (September 18, 2020), https://www.dw.com/en/us-supreme-court-justice-ruth-bader-ginsburg-a-champion-of-womens-rights/a-53384408. See also Holly Honderich and Jessica Lussenhop, "Ruth Bader Ginsburg: Obituary of the Supreme Court Justice," *BBC News* (September 18, 2020), https://www.bbc.com/news/world-us-canada-49488374.

Justice Ginsburg expressed her commitment to unequal political opportunities for men in November 2012. The following is the local news article that first reported it: "Ginsburg Wants to See All-Female Supreme Court," *CBS DC* (November 27, 2012), https://washington.cbslocal.com/2012/11/27/ginsburg-wants-to-see-all-female-supreme-court/.

# Afterword
*A Brief Note on Free Speech*

This book is an exercise in authentic free speech. No doubt, if its arguments are taken seriously by a sufficient number of people, the author will be accused of hate speech by the White Liberal Matriarchy and its male allies. If he were Canadian or a New Zealander, he could expect to face charges before an unelected Human Rights Tribunal. Such tribunals exist to impose liberal ideology and censorship on everyone by fining and/or imprisoning those brave enough to speak up against their tyranny. The current author has written this book to do his part to prevent such unelected despotism from encroaching upon the US.

How is free speech to be understood? This book's thesis has presupposed that a commitment to authentic free speech must include and protect speakers who intend to cause others real, demonstrable *harm*. If speech that harms is not protected by a commitment to "free speech," permitted speech can hardly be termed *free*. Thus, if a man refuses a woman's offer of sex and makes it clear that he does so, *because he deems her unworthy of love*, his speech must remain constitutionally protected and free. If a man refuses a transwoman's offer of sex and makes it clear that he does so, *because he does not recognize the transwoman's gender identity as valid*, his speech must also remain constitutionally protected and free. The White Liberal Matriarchy hates such speech, because it will not tolerate dissent, or anyone more generally who is out to hurt the feelings of the people the WLM feels sorry for.

But why are the White Liberal Matriarchy's members so prone to verbal violence? Why do they have such difficulty functioning in environments where their opponents have the freedom to openly disagree? The answer is what the current author terms "emotional incontinence." The White Liberal Matriarchs and their male allies know that they do not have the virtue required to repress their penchant for verbal violence when their opponents openly reject their values and make rhetorically powerful arguments that threaten truth-claims they deem to be sacred, especially truth-claims regarding human and civil rights. To ensure that their emotional incontinence is not dragged into the public's view, they have changed the rules of the game so that no one is allowed to say, write, or even think anything that might trigger a disordered emotional reaction from those who lack the emotional maturity required to remain present and to fight fairly in the midst of important disagreements.

Curiously, while writing this book, the author realized that what he calls "emotional incontinence" was termed "hysteria" by Victorians. *The Fraud of Feminism* by Ernest Bax contains a fairly lengthy description of what was understood by the term in 1913. The author encourages all and sundry to read it.[1] Although he does not endorse all of Bax's findings, in his experience the condition of not being able to restrain disordered emotions and not being able to remain present while fighting fairly in the midst of important disagreements is something women are more prone to than men. However one should term such disordered and violent emotions, it renders those who suffer them less fit for political and academic life than those of us who have the ability to remain present and to act appropriately while our opponents disagree with us for a good reason.

In sum, only if the White, Liberal Matriarchy censors men like me, can emotionally incontinent and undeservedly privileged women rule in accordance with their caprice, while shoving into a straight jacket anyone who might do, say, or write the slightest thing that might hurt their feelings and ignite their hysteria in the public's view.

---

[1] Bax, *The Fraud of Feminism*, 33–46. Available online at https://archive.org/details/fraudoffeminism00baxerich/page/32/mode/2up. Happily, the book has been reprinted as Ernest Belfort Bax, *The Fraud of Feminism* (Fairford: Echo Library, 2016).

*Maximilian Hanlon resides somewhere in the American Midwest and intends to become a lawyer to sue the right people. He would like to hear from those who wish to join in the fight against the White Liberal Matriarchy and may be reached at Maximilian.Hanlon.PhD@gmail.com.*

www.ingramcontent.com/pod-product-compliance
Lightning Source LLC
Chambersburg PA
CBHW021342290326
41933CB00037B/340